BRIGHT NOTES

THE MAJOR PLAYS OF HENRIK IBSEN

Intelligent Education

Nashville, Tennessee

BRIGHT NOTES: The Major Plays of Henrik Ibsen
www.BrightNotes.com

No part of this publication may be used or reproduced in any manner whatsoever without written permission, except in the case of brief quotations in critical articles and reviews. For permissions, contact Influence Publishers http://www.influencepublishers.com.

ISBN: 978-1-645424-48-2 (Paperback)
ISBN: 978-1-645424-49-9 (eBook)

Published in accordance with the U.S. Copyright Office Orphan Works and Mass Digitization report of the register of copyrights, June 2015.

Originally published by Monarch Press.
Edward T. Byrnes; Stanley Brodwin, 1965
2020 Edition published by Influence Publishers.

Interior design by Lapiz Digital Services. Cover Design by Thinkpen Designs.

Printed in the United States of America.

Library of Congress Cataloging-in-Publication Data forthcoming.
Names: Intelligent Education
Title: BRIGHT NOTES: The Major Plays of Henrik Ibsen
Subject: STU004000 STUDY AIDS / Book Notes

CONTENTS

1)	Introduction to Henrik Ibsen	1
2)	Introduction to Brand	10
3)	Brand: Textual Analysis	13
	Act One	13
	Act Two	15
	Act Three	18
	Act Four	22
	Act Five	25
4)	Brand: Character Analyses	32
5)	Introduction to Peer Gynt	35
6)	Peer Gynt: Textual Analysis	39
	Act One	39
	Act Two	42
	Act Three	47
	Act Four	50
	Act Five	54

7)	Peer Gynt: Character Analyses	62
8)	Introduction to A Doll's House	64
9)	A Doll's House: Textual Analysis	67
	Act One	67
	Act Two	71
	Act Three	74
10)	A Doll's House: Character Analyses	78
11)	Introduction to Ghosts	81
12)	Ghosts: Textual Analysis	83
	Act One	83
	Act Two	86
	Act Three	90
13)	Ghosts: Character Analyses	93
14)	Introduction to An Enemy of The People	96
15)	An Enemy of The Peoples: Textual Analysis	99
	Act One	99
	Act Two	102
	Act Three	105
	Act Four	108
	Act Five	111
16)	An Enemy of The Peoples: Character Analyses	115
17)	Introduction to The Wild Duck	117

18)	The Wild Duck: Textual Analysis	120
	Act One	120
	Act Two	123
	Act Three	126
	Act Four	129
	Act Five	132
19)	The Wild Duck: Character Analyses	136
20)	Introduction to Hedda Gabler	139
21)	Hedda Gabler: Textual Analysis	142
	Act One	142
	Act Two	146
	Act Three	150
	Act Four	153
22)	Hedda Gabler: Character Analyses	157
23)	Introduction to The Master Builder	160
24)	The Master Builder: Textual Analysis	162
	Act One	162
	Act Two	166
	Act Three	169
25)	The Master Builder: Character Analyses	172
26)	Introduction to Pillars of Society	174
27)	Pillars of Society: Textual Analysis	176
	Act One	176
	Act Two	178

	Act Three	180
	Act Four	182
28)	Introduction to Rosmersholm	185
29)	Rosmersholm: Textual Analysis	187
	Act One	187
	Act Two	189
	Act Three	191
	Act Four	192
30)	Introduction to John Gabriel Borkman	195
31)	John Gabriel Borkman: Textual Analysis	197
	Act One	197
	Act Two	199
	Act Three	201
	Act Four	203
32)	Critical Commentary	206
33)	Essay Questions and Answers	210
34)	Bibliography and Guide to Further Research	217

HENRIK IBSEN

INTRODUCTION

IBSEN'S EARLY YEARS

Henrik Ibsen was born in Skien, a small coastal town in Southern Norway, on March 20, 1828. At first a prosperous merchant, his father went into bankruptcy in 1836. In that year the family moved to a small farm north of the town where they lived in poverty. Young Henrik was compelled to attend a small local school where, in company with other poor children, he received an inferior education. In 1843 the family returned to town, but still lived in what to Ibsen was a humiliating poverty. In the following year, he left home to become a druggist's apprentice in another small town, Grimstad. He visited his family only once afterwards, in 1852. The poverty of these early years left its mark, for Ibsen, resentful of his early life and of his family, became stubborn, rebellious, and often aloof and unsociable.

IBSEN'S YOUTH

Ibsen rebelled against conventions, although he performed his duties adequately at the druggist's. With several other youths, he formed a radical club, dedicated to the cause of Scandinavian unity and freedom, and critical of the times in general. Ibsen showed his revolt against small-town life by numerous practical jokes, by heavy drinking and gambling, and by fathering an illegitimate child when he was only eighteen.

Encouraged by his friends, he began to write at first inflammatory patriotic verses inspired by the unsuccessful revolts in Hungary and Germany in 1848. By 1850 he had written his first play, *Catiline*, while he was studying for entrance examinations at the University of Christiania (now Oslo). After his failure to complete the examinations, he continued to write verse, and began to produce satiric articles for several liberal publications. He then joined a secret revolutionary party which was soon dissolved by government action. Never did Ibsen again engage actively in any political party.

IBSEN AND THE NORWEGIAN THEATRE

Ibsen's miscellaneous writings soon attracted the attention of the great violinist Ole Bull, who secured for the young author the position of theatre poet and stage manager (now called director) at the theatre in Bergen. Here from 1851 to 1857 Ibsen staged and directed nearly 150 performances of different plays by Shakespeare, the industrious 19th-century French playwright Eugene Scribe, and others. In addition, he wrote several pieces, of which the *Feast at Solhoug* (1855), a romantic historical drama, is most notable.

In 1856 he proposed to Susannah Thoresen, whom he married two years later. In 1857, he moved to Christiania (Oslo), where he became director of the Norwegian Theatre. Here his career seems to have reached a point of indecision, since he neglected both writing and the theatre, plunging into social life with his literary friends, and drinking heavily. After the bankruptcy of the Norwegian Theatre in 1862, Ibsen, depressed and nearly desperate, was sometimes seen drunk on the streets of Christiania. A brief success with the drama *The Pretenders* (1863) inspired him to write a number of poems, but he became bitterly disappointed with current political events, especially with the failure of the Norwegians to help the Danes in their unsuccessful war against Prussia in 1863. He left his native country in 1864, to remain a voluntary exile until 1891.

IBSEN'S YEARS OF EXILE

In Italy, Ibsen composed his first truly great work, the faulty but magnificently conceived *Brand* (1866). So well was the play received that it was frequently reprinted, and the Norwegian parliament voted Ibsen a pension for life. Relieved of financial pressures, he was able to devote more attention to writing. Having produced in *Brand* the portrait of an ideal reformer, he next presented the world with *Peer Gynt* (1867), the drama of a careless, self-indulgent fortune-seeker. Both of these verse dramas are distinguished by some of Ibsen's best dramatic poetry. After *Peer Gynt*, Ibsen wrote only two more plays in verse, the sprawling historical narrative *Emperor and Galilean* (1873) about the Roman Emperor Julian the Apostate (who reigned from 361-363 A.D.), and *When We Dead Awaken* (1899), his last attempt at playwriting.

After *Emperor and Galilean*, Ibsen turned to realistic prose drama dealing with contemporary problems. From 1877 to 1881, he steadily produced, every other year, one drama after another. The popular success of the first of these, *Pillars of Society* (1877), led to his receiving an honorary doctorate from the University of Upsala in Sweden. But two years later, his iconoclastic *A Doll's House* made him the enemy of conservatives everywhere. So great was the uproar that Ibsen was compelled to compose an alternative and less offensive ending, in which the wife, Nora, returns to her husband. The next play, *Ghosts* (1881), with its treatment of venereal disease, outraged even those who could accept *A Doll's House* without the alternate ending. Ibsen rapidly followed with *An Enemy of the People* (1882), a comedy depicting a rather bumbling but well-intentioned reformer. In the next decade, Ibsen wrote a play every other year, ending with *The Master Builder* (1892). After this play, his genius faltered in *Little Eyolf* (1894), came to life brilliantly in *John Gabriel Borkman* (1896), and presented its dying embers in *When We Dead Awaken* (1899).

IBSEN'S LAST YEARS

In 1891, Ibsen returned to Norway and settled in Christiania, where he lived a quiet retired life. In 1900, a severe stroke left him an invalid until his death on May 23, 1906.

IBSEN'S PERSONALITY

Stubborn and aloof in his earlier years, Ibsen, once he became famous, developed a reputation for being difficult of access. His wife protected him from would-be interviewers, and he himself would seldom either visit people or entertain. On rare occasions he would go to the theatre to see one of his own plays, but never would he attend a concert or an opera. Yet he was fond of hearing from his wife and son of their visits to friends and of their frequent attendance at theatres, which he encouraged. He never cultivated friendships, but he allowed friends, at times, to cultivate him. As he said to the famous Danish critic Georg

Brandes, "Friends are a costly luxury." In late years he was in his personal appearance and conservative way of life the complete opposite of the iconoclastic freethinker that contemporary critics of his plays considered him to be.

IBSEN'S HISTORICAL BACKGROUNDS

Almost alone among European countries, Norway after 1814 enjoyed a large measure of independence. Separated in that year from Denmark and joined to the monarchy of Sweden, Norway had its own constitution, which provided for an executive branch, comprised of appointed civil servants (like the Mayor in *Brand*), a legislature elected indirectly by the people, and a separate judiciary. Hence when revolutions broke out all over Europe in 1848, Norway was spared rebellion, although it had its share of revolutionary and radical organizations. To the most influential of these, led by Marcus Moller Thrane, Ibsen for a brief period belonged, but the arrest and imprisonment of Thrane and his assistants convinced him to give up active politics. For the liberal socialist views of Thrane and others, Ibsen in later life had little use; he seems largely indifferent to the problems of labor, and in general, avoids presenting people of the lower classes in his plays. What these events did do for Ibsen was to intensify his spirit of rebellion against authority and against entrenched opinions - **themes** which appear later in *Ghosts* (1881) and *An Enemy of the People* (1882) as well as in other plays.

IBSEN'S LITERARY BACKGROUNDS

The language and literature of Norway was Dano-Norwegian. Although a Norwegian state had been firmly established by the constitution of 1814, Norwegian literature was still practically identical with Danish. The official language of Norway, Dano-Norwegian, was virtually the same as Danish. Although there had been a number of earlier Norwegian authors, especially the famous dramatist Ludvig Holberg (1684 - 1754), often referred to as "the Moliere of the North," all of them, including Holberg, had spent most of their lives in Denmark. Indeed a Norwegian literary society established in 1772 met regularly in Copenhagen, the Danish capital. Hence for Ibsen's immediate literary backgrounds we must look to Danish and to general European literature. Two writers may be singled out as having particular influence on Ibsen: the Danish romantic poet Adam Gottlob Oehlenschlager (1779 - 1850), whose romantic plays celebrating the Scandinavian era of the Vikings (8th to 11th centuries) inspired Ibsen's earlier works; and the French playwright Eugene Scribe (1791 - 1861), at least a dozen of whose more than 400 plays Ibsen produced while he was a theatre poet and manager.

IBSEN'S DRAMATIC CAREER

Ibsen's total dramatic output readily lends itself to a threepart division:

Romantic Period, 1850 to 1873

The greatest works of this period are the two verse dramas *Brand* (1866) and *Peer Gynt* (1867), which, although romantic in vitality and poetry, especially in the idealism of the former and the lyricism of the latter, form a transition to Ibsen's later work, since they bitterly denounce the moral sloth of his contemporaries. Several other plays with satiric content date from this period, particularly *Love's Comedy* (1862), but the majority of plays in these years are romantic historical dramas. The best of these show considerable debt to the French dramatist Eugene Scribe (see above and Bibliography, under Stanton): *Lady Inger of Ostraat* (1855), a powerful romantic drama of intrigue that gives promise of Ibsen's later mastery of psychological problems; and *The Vikings of Helgeland* (1858), a simple, elemental, yet moving tragedy. This period ends with the massive drama *Emperor and Galilean* (1873), which, like the first play of the period, *Catiline* (1850), betrays Ibsen's impatience with traditional attitudes and values, since in each play he sympathizes with historical characters famous for rebellion, either politically like *Catiline* (fl. 68-62 B.C.) or religiously like Julian the Apostate (361-363 A.D.).

Realistic Period, 1877 to 1890

With *Pillars of Society* (1877), Ibsen launched a series of plays dealing with either social problems, as *A Doll's House* (1879) and *Ghosts* (1881), or psychological problems, as *The Lady from the Seas* (1888) and *Hedda Gabler* (1890). In the eight plays of this period, Ibsen both originated and brought to perfection the problem play or thesis play. All of these plays are concerned with contemporary life, in completely realistic settings. The symbolism that studded the texts of *Brand* and *Peer Gynt* is now almost completely lacking. Instead, Ibsen chose to present his **themes** or "problems" to the audience through the medium of realistic characters and straightforward plots. Two of the plays, however, recall the earlier masterpieces in their use of symbolism: *Rosmersholm* (1886) and *The Lady from the Sea* (1888). In all of the plays of this period, Ibsen deals directly or indirectly with the theme of the individual attempting to realize himself in the face of established conventions. This is as true of Nora in *A Doll's House* as it is in *Hedda Gabler*.

Symbolist Period, 1892 to 1899

The four plays in this period all present a realization of defeat. Now in his sixties and settled again in Norway, Ibsen could look back over his career, but apparently he was not satisfied. The best of these plays, *The Master Builder* (1892), deals with an aging architect who, having renounced love and therefore life as well to devote himself to his art, now goes down to defeat before the new generation. The same **theme** is presented in the three subsequent plays, especially in *John Gabriel Borkman* (1896), a drama of a financier who sacrifices his love to concentrate on amassing a fortune. He realizes too late the truth of *Brand*'s contention that "to live is an art." Both plays suffer from the same defect - an excessive weight of symbolism that all but crushes the dramatic action.

Ibsen's last play, *When We Dead Awaken* (1899), is, despite its weakness as a drama and the colorlessness of much of its verse, a fitting conclusion to his career in virtue of its **theme**. "When we dead awaken," he asks in the play, "what do we see then? We see that we have never lived." In this play, as in all of his plays since *Brand*, Ibsen defended the individual against all conditions developments in modern society that tended to detract from one's pursuit of freedom and happiness. Ibsen remained to the last a champion of the individual against the encroachments of society.

IBSEN AND THE PROBLEM PLAY

More than any other playwright of the 19th century, Ibsen is to be credited with the origin and development of the problem play or drama of ideas. This term "problem play" refers specifically to that type of drama which Ibsen wrote starting with *Pillars of Society* (1877). In this sort play, the chief emphasis is on the presentation of a social or psychological problem through the medium of a drama. Therefore, characterization and plot structure are often subordinated to the **theme**. It must not be thought, however, that the problem play loses anything in effectiveness because of this emphasis on **theme**. Ibsen wrote powerful dramas in which the emotional impact usually tends to underscore the immediacy of the **theme** or problem. But although Ibsen presents problems, he rarely gives solutions. "A dramatist's business," he always said, "is not to answer questions, but only to ask them."

BRAND

INTRODUCTION

To understand *Brand*, one must remember that Ibsen reflects in this play as in *Peer Gynt* some of the ideas of the Danish philosopher Soren Kierkegaard (1813-1855). Ibsen himself disclaimed any knowledge of Kierkegaard, saying that he "had read very little and understood even less" of the philosopher's writings. But several of Ibsen's friends at Grimstad were well acquainted with Kierkegaard's work, and Ibsen's own wife, Susannah Thoresen, learned about it from her stepmother, who was an ardent follower of Kierkergaard.

Certain of the philosopher's basic ideas seem most influential in *Brand*:

1. The strict, austere concept of Christianity as absolutely "Christ-like."

2. A contempt for any sort of moral or spiritual compromise.

3. The importance of spiritual ideals: the "absolute ideal demand,"

4. A conviction that martyrdom is essential to Christianity; that is, that a man is most Christian when he is dead. To Kierkegaard and his followers, this was the basic paradox of Christianity.

5. A contempt for the modern clergy as being unChristian and self-seeking.

6. The supreme power and importance of man's free will to choose either good or evil.

7. The supreme importance of the individual (Kierkegaard always insisted that a man "be himself").

These ideas contributed to make Kierkegaard a supreme example of the idealistic philosopher both for his age and for our own.

The play was written in Italy in the summer of 1865, in less than three and one-half months. It was published in March, 1866, and went into three more editions within a year. This play and the next, *Peer Gynt*, represent Ibsen's most successful efforts in verse drama, both from a financial and from a literary point of view.

Brand is the drama of a strong-willed man who persists in following what to him is the right way of life, and who in spite of all temptations and obstacles insists on trying to fulfill his impossible ideal of "all or nothing." Regardless of consequences, Brand must lead his people to the heights. The end for such an extremist must be catastrophe.

The melodious verse of the original contributes to the effectiveness of the piece as a dramatic poem. As a stage drama it is difficult to present. In fact, its premier performance was in Stockholm, Sweden, in 1895, twenty-nine years after its publication, Properly abridged, however, *Brand* never fails to impress audiences with its tragic denunciation of moral apathy.

CHARACTERS

Brand, a parson.

His Mother.

Peasant And Son.

Einar, an artist, later a missionary.

Agnes, his bride, then Brand's.

Gerd, a gypsy girl.

The Mayor.

The Sexton, the clerk of the parsonage.

Peasants.

The Doctor.

The Schoolmaster.

The Dean.

BRAND

TEXTUAL ANALYSIS

ACT ONE

ACT ONE, SCENE ONE

Act One, Scene One (a wild snowy field). Brand walks across the field, which is extremely dangerous because of streams undermining the snow. A peasant and his son try to make Brand turn back, but he continues despite their cries of danger. They return, while Brand climbs higher, meditating on the difference between what things are and what they ought to be.

The fog and snow clear, and a bright summer morning breaks through. Two young lovers, Einar and Agnes, appear. Brand warns them of the precipice near which they stand, but in their joy in life and in each other they are indifferent to their danger. Einar and Brand recognizes each other as former classmates.

Brand speaks of Einar's God of love and joy as being dead. He does not blame Einar for being joyous, but he insists that he be joyous "wholly and entirely, and not by pieces." Brand describes his God as stormy, inexorable, all-loving, youthful entirely unlike the God of the present slack generation. His parting words are "Remember, life is an art."

ACT ONE, SCENE TWO

Act One, Scene Two (a path along a bluff). Brand meets Gerd, the young gypsy girl, who tells him of the "Ice Church," a wild and dangerous chasm far in the hills, and of the hawk, which she wants to strike out against. Inspired by what he has seen and heard, Brand sees his mission as a quest against the lighthearted, fainthearted, and wronghearted.

Comment

The **exposition** present the fiercely determined Brand, who moves on over the snow and ice heedless of danger and unmindful of his bleeding feet. The contrast between Brand's inexorable idealism and the carefree joyfulness of Einar and Agnes is obvious. Two symbols are introduced at the end of the act: the Ice Church, which is Gerd's refuge from evil; and the hawk, which seems to represent a harsh element in Brand's quest as well as in Gerd's life. It is significant that Gerd attempts to fight against and to fly from this evil symbol, while Brand not yet seen it.

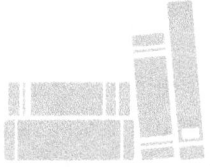

BRAND

TEXTUAL ANALYSIS

ACT TWO

ACT TWO, SCENE ONE

Act Two, Scene One (a church by a fjord). To alleviate a famine, the Mayor distributes food to the people while Brand speaks to them, telling them that the misery and horror of the famine are for their spiritual benefit, that "necessity breeds ... heroism." A strange woman comes from across the fjord, seeking Brand's help for her husband, who, having slain his sick child, is now in danger of losing his own soul. Brand asks for a volunteer to assist him in crossing the fjord by boat, but no one will do so because of the storm that rages over the water. Finally, Agnes leaves Einar to follow Brand and they cross safely despite the wind and rough water.

ACT TWO, SCENE ONE

Act Two, Scene One (a hut on a point over the fjord). Brand is approached by several peasants who offer help, but he answers:

"If you have given everything but life, know that you have given nothing." The spokesman for the peasants asks Brand to be their pastor, but Brand envisions a wider calling. The man asks for guidance and is told: "If you cannot be what you ought, then be wholly what you can."

Brand's mother appears, ordering rather than asking him to be careful of his life and then of his inheritance after she dies, for she has devoted her life to amassing a legacy for him. Brand recalls to her an incident from his childhood, when he observed her ransacking the room where her husband, Brand's father, lay dead. She was looking for whatever treasure was left to her. Brand's mother then recalls how she took her father's advice and married for money rather than for love. Brand reminds her that she gave her soul away as part of that bargain, and that to pass on a legacy is no way to purchase immortality. He agrees to take on her spiritual debts, but must leave her with her own burden of guilt, to be paid for only by repentance. He agrees to come to her at the moment of her death, but only if she will give away everything that binds her to earth, that is, her fortune. She is willing to give away much, but she cannot bear to part with all. Brand insists on "all or nothing."

Brand determines to become pastor of the little church by the fjord mainly because his duty demands that he remain near his mother to await her call. Einar comes along to bring Agnes away with him, but she decides to stay with Brand despite Einar's discouragement and the Parson's hardness, for, as he tells her, he requires "all or nothing."

Comment

In the first act we saw Brand fighting the passive dangers of ice and snow, here we see him successfully combat the active danger of the storm-tossed fjord. Both actions are typical of the iron-willed man who performs what he considers his duty without regard to danger. His message to the people is representative of Kierkegaardian thought: the idea that fear and suffering are spiritually beneficial.

Equally in tune with the Danish philosopher is Brand's exhortation to the peasants in the second scene to be "wholly what you can." It recalls Kierkegaard's "Be yourself." Brand's inflexible determination is again displayed in the scene with his mother, when he demands not only "much" but "all or nothing."

Of great interest to us is Brand's telling of the incident from his childhood, for it obviously made a great impression on him. Particularly significant is the coldness of the home without love, for his mother's only passion seems to have been money. This loveless childhood formed Brand into the cold, hard, determined man of God that he is.

BRAND

TEXTUAL ANALYSIS

ACT THREE

Act Three (three years later, the parsonage garden). Brand awaits patiently the call from his mother. He tells Agnes how he never knew love unit his marriage, because his childhood was bleak and without affection. Agnes remarks that his love is hard; he agrees, insisting that he knows God's love, which is unmoved even by the terror that all mankind must sooner or later experience. Again Brand insists that man avoid compromise, for if he works half-heartedly or without thoroughness he is doomed.

The Doctor enters on his way to visit Brand's mother. He asks the Parson to come along but the latter refuses because his mother has not yet sent for him. The Doctor rebukes Brand for being excessive in will but deficient in love. The Parson answers that the word "love" is overused; that before true love, the will must satisfy the demand of the ideal, the demand that we all will the supreme sacrifice of "all or nothing."

Two messengers come from Brand's mother: the first offers one-half of her goods; the second, a little later, nine-tenths. Brand refuses, despite his mental anguish over the decision. He seems to doubt for a moment not his ideals or his refusal to see his mother, but his own decision to remain at the Parsonage. He feels that he really made no sacrifice in giving up what he felt was his call to take over such a small church. He is also concerned for the health of his infant son, Alf, who seems to have a fever. The thought that God might demand his son for a sacrifice then occurs to him.

The Mayor comes in, telling Brand how rich the latter will be as soon as his mother dies. The Mayor suggests that Brand leave the area, since his ideas are too big for the poor people of the neighborhood. The Parson refuses to leave, and threatens to bring about a spiritual uprising, a war against lowness and pettiness. He then informs the Mayor that he has the best of the people with him. The official agrees, but answers confidently that he, in turn, has most of the people on his side.

The Doctor returns, bringing news of the death of Brand's mother. Grief-stricken, Brand still summons all his determination and strong will to reject the Doctor's plea that he be humane. Brand cries out against the humanitarianism of his contemporaries, who conceal their moral cowardice under the guise of humaneness.

The Doctor examines Alf, and tells Agnes and Brand that they must leave the parsonage where the sun never shines. Nearly wild with fear for his son, Brand is ready to depart, but first the Doctor and then a peasant throw his own words "all or nothing" back at him. The wild gipsy girl Gerd enters, telling how the Parson is running away. She sees Alf and refers to him as an idol. Agnes and Brand decide to stay, realizing that by so doing they are sacrificing their son.

Comment

Consistently throughout this act, Brand, at the cost of great personal agony, stifles whatever emotions might turn him away from his duty. His remarks about his own bleak childhood are of interest, since the cold, loveless times of his youth are paralleled by the symbolism of the bleak, cold, parsonage on which the sun never shines. The sunless parsonage also represents the cold and seemingly emotionless will that drives Brand on.

But Brand is anything but free from emotion. The dramatic effectiveness of the act is enhanced by the two emotional crises through which he must pass - the death of his mother and the sacrifice of his child. In each case we see Brand in agony, but in each case his iron will suppresses his emotions and impels him forward. In each instance Ibsen uses **foreshadowing** to heighten the tragic effect. The warning of the Doctor and the messengers suggests what is to follow: the death of Brand's mother unattended by her son. Likewise, Brand's own thought, when he first sees his son's illness, that his son might be demanded as a sacrifice, anticipates the final scene of the act.

Brand's outcry against humanitarianism must be considered in the light of nineteenth-century Scandinavia. Ibsen had in mind particularly the shallow humanitarianism represented by the Mayor, who prides himself on relieving the conditions of famine we observed in Act Two, scene one. In this play, as in others, Ibsen sharply criticizes the shallowness and hypocrisy of civil servants in his native country.

The label "idol" which Gerd gives to the child Alf will reappear in the fourth act, when Brand adopts the term himself. It shakes Brand's resolution to depart even more than did the words of the Doctor or the peasant.

BRAND

TEXTUAL ANALYSIS

ACT FOUR

Act Four (the parsonage on Christmas Eve). Agnes is dressed in black grieving for the death of their son. Brand gives her little comfort; she must dry her tears and go about her work. Brand insists on referring to the remains of Alf buried in the churchyard as a corpse, while to Agnes it is still Alf. Agnes feels the need of some sort of comfort, for everything about Brand is too great at times for her, except for the little church, which seems far too small. Brand then recalls Gerd's jibes about the ugly little church, and the remarks of many in the district about its small size. He determines to build a newer and larger church.

The Mayor enters, spouting humanitarian sentiments, and is desirous of effecting a reconciliation with Brand. In order to regain some of his lost popularity, the Mayor has decided to build a home for paupers, which will also have room for lunatics, if necessary. He needs Brand's support in order to complete his project, but the Parson announces his own intention of building. The Mayor at first opposes, but when he sees that Brand intends to pay for the costs out of his own inheritance, the official realizes that he must join Brand, whose generosity will make him popular. As he leaves, the Mayor mentions that Gerd is the child of the rejected suitor of Brand's mother.

Brand meditates upon the need for self-sacrifice, the only way, as he sees it, for people to rise spiritually. He thinks of his sacrifice of his own child, and of his prayers, and wonders if God heard them. He can find no answers Agnes enters and looks out the window at the churchyard where Alf is buried. Brand chides her for paying attention to an "idol." He suggests that her thinking still of Alf renders her sacrifice invalid; because she has not yet given all of her child, she still retains memories. While Brand retires to his study, Agnes reflects on her dead child, then takes some of Alf's clothes out of a drawer, holds them up, and looks at them fondly. Brand sees her, yet cannot bring himself to make her give up what he considers her last idol. A gipsy woman comes to the door, begging garments for her little child. Brand orders Agnes to give up Alf's clothes. She resists, calling it "sacrilege," and then agrees to give part. Brand demands all or nothing and she complies reluctantly. But once she has given up all, she feels a sense of freedom and sees a vision of Alf at the throne of God. She reminds Brand of the saying, "He who sees Jehovah shall die." Agnes thanks Brand for leading her to victory, and Brand concludes with the enigmatic remark that to lose all is to gain all.

Comment

Brand's refusal to comfort Agnes is in line with the harshness and severity of his ideals. His determination to build a new church represents his goal of spiritually elevating his flock. The ugly little church on which the sun never shines has a twofold significance. First and most important, it represents contemporary Christianity, shrunken and sunless in its spiritual apathy. Secondly, and conversely, the lack of sunlight also suggests Brand's own coldness and austerity. The justice of Brand's denunciation of humanitarianism in the third act becomes much more apparent when we witness the Mayor's repeated appeal to the humanitarianism of the times, when no one is called upon to sacrifice more than a modest sum of money. His attitude, when compared to Brand's, seems nearly contemptible, even though it was the attitude of many of Ibsen's contemporaries. The Mayor's opportunism is also evident in his readiness to join what he considers the winning side.

Brand seems cruel in driving Agnes to give up all relics of Alf, yet the resulting liberation of Agnes' spirit seems to justify his attitude. Her spiritual freedom here represents a purification of herself, a rising above her more human-Eve like imperfections, just as Brand's quest involves a similar purification of his Adam-like qualities. But the Kierkegaardian paradox, that a man is most Christian when he is dead, appears to be exemplified here. When Agnes is most Christ-like, she obviously, by her own vision, is near death.

The final lines of this act relate a similar paradox. When Brand states that to lose all is to gain all, he repeats the central conviction of Kierkegaard, that martyrdom is essential to Christianity. Accordingly, Agnes and then Brand, when they lose all, even their lives, on the physical level, gain immortality on the spiritual.

BRAND

TEXTUAL ANALYSIS

ACT FIVE

ACT FIVE, SCENE ONE

Act Five, Scene One (six months later, before the new church). The Sexton and the Schoolmaster discuss the great activity in the district caused by the enthusiasm over the building of the new church. When asked about the possible future of the area, the Schoolmaster answers that the future never comes, because once it comes, it is past. They both feel sympathy for Brand since the death of his wife, but as officials they consider it necessary to stifle their personal feelings, following the lead of the Mayor whom they both admire.

The organ music, which has sounded low during the preceding conversation, suddenly breaks into a roar and ends in a piercing discord. Brand enters, complaining that the organ has lost its power of speech in the new church. The new building oppresses and drives down the organ, shutting in the melody.

The Mayor enters, beaming with pride and satisfaction. When Brand remarks that the new church, as it stands, is small, the Mayor objects that it is big enough for the people of the district, and he insists that Brand make no derogatory remarks about its size. Brand counters that greatness is not measured merely by size, but the Mayor is unable to comprehend.

The Dean arrives, full of enthusiasm for the new church, his sermon, and the delicious banquet. He warns Brand that the new church, since it was donated to the State, must be used to serve the State. He criticizes Brand for devoting too much time to individuals in his parish, and not enough to the more important matter of treating all alike, so as to level off inequalities and make all church-goers equal. The Dean makes it quite clear that Brand, as a civil servant, must serve the aims of the State as well as the official State Church. The Dean continues by denouncing individualism as detrimental to society: "When God wills a man to fall, He first makes him an individual." To Brand's objection that death is not destruction, the Dean answers that life and faith only prosper when kept apart. Brand refuses to betray his ideals, and the Dean agrees. He tells the Parson not to betray them, just to keep them to himself. When the Dean ends by saying that the age is humanitarian, Brand orders him away.

Alone in his idealism, Brand craves to meet even one person who can understand him and assure him. Einar, the artist of the first act, enters, pale and thin and dressed in black. He tells Brand of his conversion from a life of gambling and drunkenness to a life of faith. He first became a Total Abstinence preacher, but because of the numerous temptations in such a life, he now decides to become a missionary in Africa. He has no interest in hearing of Agnes, except of her death. To Einar, Agnes was doomed because her faith, like Brand's, was unmoved. The latter also, according to the artist, is doomed. Einar departs, boasting of his own purity and atonement through prayer.

The people rush to the Church to hear Brand speak. He addresses them on the error of building such a church, since not merely a larger building was required, but rather larger souls capable of the supreme sacrifice of "all or nothing." He condemns the spirit of compromise that the new church represents both to the Mayor and to the Dean. Brand rejects the church of compromise, of Sundays only, and recommends to the people the great church of life, a church large enough to embrace all rather than just a part of them. He locks the church and throws away the key, then leads the crowd away. The Mayor and the Dean follow to try to recover control of the people.

Comment

The Sexton and the Schoolmaster are glib but shallow characters, pale reflections of the shrewd Mayor. The Schoolmaster's quibble about the future never coming affords him a good excuse for not keeping promises. When Brand then cannot soar heavenward in his organ-playing, we are not amazed, since the new church was built largely through the influence and cooperation of the materialistic local officials.

The Mayor and the Dean are also complementary characters. Both are concerned largely with making the day a success, that is, with having everything go smoothly. The statements of the Dean with regard to equality and individualism are typical of mid-nineteenth-century Scandinavian bureaucrats, to whom keeping the people in line and the government running smoothly are the most important considerations.

The Dean, of course, as a higher official in the State Church, looks upon himself as more of a civil servant than a churchman; hence his rather irreligious insistence on keeping life and faith separate. Ibsen adds to his character by picturing him as a lover of fine food, infatuated with the sound of his own voice. In contrast to Brand, he is a shallow, self-seeking compromiser.

Brand's meeting with Einar at first seems difficult to interpret, mainly because of the latter's denunciation of the Parson. But the emotionalism and perhaps even hypocrisy of the erstwhile artist is suggested by his rapid transfer from Total Abstinence to missionary work, and even more by his insistence on Agnes' and Brand's doom and his own salvation.

Brand's decision to lead the people up into the mountains is triggered chiefly by the Mayor's and the Dean's insistence on compromise. It is interesting to note that the Ice Church to which Brand tries to lead the people is the gipsy girl Gerd's own church of life. The connection between Brand and Gerd noticed in Acts One and Four is thus furthered, anticipating the last scene of the play.

ACT FIVE, SCENE TWO

Act Five, Scene Two (a farm high in the hills). Brand leads the people up into the hills, but they begin to grow tired and hungry. They ask for food, then for an accounting of how long the struggle Brand speaks of will last, what it will cost them, and how much they will gain. Brand demands from them the ultimate sacrifice of will - "all or nothing." Disappointed, the crowd begins to turn on Brand, and, encouraged by the apparent kindness and indulgence of the Dean and the Mayor, as well as by a trick of the latter's, they cry out against Brand, driving him over the wastelands, and stoning him. The crowd is very thankful to the two officials, who are praised for their "Christian charity" and "popular manners." Brand is seen far in the distance struggling onward with the gipsy Gerd at his heels.

ACT FIVE, SCENE THREE

Act Five, Scene Three (the wasteland, beneath high peaks). In a long monologue, Brand reflects on the cowardice of those afraid to make a sacrifice, on their moral wretchedness, weakness, and insignificance. Through the storm, an unseen choir murmurs that Brand is doomed, that he will never be like "Him" (that is, like Christ). In a vision, Agnes appears, and tells him that all will be well if only he forgets three words, "all or nothing." Brand refuses, for he must continue his quest for realization of the ideal; he must make whatever sacrifice is demanded of him. The figure disappears, with a shrill cry, "Die, the world has no use for you!" Brand feels that the figure was the spirit of compromise.

Gerd comes along, carrying a rifle with which she plans to kill the hawk mentioned in Act One, scene two. She reminds Brand that he is now standing in what the local people call the Ice Church, a dangerous chasm of ice. Filled with an intense longing for light and sun, Brand calls upon the name of Jesus. Gerd sees the hawk above and fires, bringing down an avalanche that buries them both and fills the whole Ice Church. A voice is heard through the noise: "He is the God of Love."

Comment

The reaction of the crowd in scene two is typical of humanity everywhere. When asked to fight, man wants to know how much and what for. The crowd's stoning of Brand is also typical, since he represents an extreme idealism that is difficult if not impossible to follow. Ironically, the two venal officials of church and state - the Dean and the Mayor - are praised by the people for their Christian virtues.

The message of the unseen chorus, that Brand will never be like Christ, is a statement of the impossibility or near-impossibility of the Parson's quest. It also prepares the reader and audience for the identification of Brand with a Christ-image a little later. The vision of Agnes that next appears seems to present a further rejection of Brand's position. But the final line of the play is the clearest denunciation of what Brand stands for: "He is the God of Love" - in the original, "Han er deus caritatis." We should recall that what Agnes wanted was a God of love or charity, and that the Doctor found Brand lacking in this essential Christian characteristic. Following Kierkegaard, Brand's own concept of God appears stern and forbidding. Hence, no matter how one attempts to interpret this line - and the attempts are numerous - one is forced to the conclusion that it represents some sort of rejection of the central philosophic position of both Kierkegaard and Brand.

The tragedy, nevertheless, is Brand's, and it is rendered perhaps more poignant by this final rejection of his "all or nothing" philosophy. He possibly begins to realize that he may have been in error when he finally sees the hawk: "Yes, this time I saw him." The hawk may represent a savage or harsh element in Brand's philosophy, which he now at last perceives. It is significant that once Brand sees the hawk, he is able both to weep and to pray. To Gerd he appears with wounded hands and bleeding forehead; in other words, a Christ-image, thus completing the identification suggested but rejected by the unseen choir. This presentation of Brand as a Christ-figure, by counterbalancing the rejection of his philosophy, tends to restore some of the balance needed for an effective tragic conclusion. If the harsh judgment of the Agnes image were to stand without anything to counterbalance it, Ibsen would, in effect, have undercut much of the effectiveness of his play.

In certain respects, this play bears comparison with classical tragedy. The conclusion is brought about largely as a result of Brand's driving, iron-willed character. Critics from Aristotle on speak of the tragic flaw, a central weakness or fault in a character that causes or contributes to his destruction. Brand's tragic flaw is his determination to follow his creed of "all or nothing," a determination that borders upon the hybris or hubris of classical Greek tragedy - the excessive pride or ambition that brings about the downfall of a great man. Spiritually, Brand is great, but his hybris causes his tragic end.

BRAND

CHARACTER ANALYSES

BRAND

Brand is a parson in the State Church. He is determined, strong-willed, and inflexible in the pursuit of his ideal. Broadly speaking, this ideal is best expressed in his favorite saying, "all or nothing," signifying a total sacrifice of the individual. Thus Brand tends to reflect the Kierkegaardian paradox of Christianity - that, martyrdom being essential, a man is most Christian when he is dead. Brand, however, is a true tragic figure in that he finally comes to a realization of his own excessive ambition or pride, his tragic flaw that brings about the death of his son and his wife, as well as his own. His determined will seems to stamp out all of his human emotions, yet much of the tragic intensity of the play stems from the tension between his will and his human feelings.

AGNES

Agnes, Brand's wife, is a young woman of an idealism second only to his. She has, however, one quality that Brand lacks - the ability to love with sympathy and tenderness rather than just with an act of the will as Brand appears to do. In addition, she longs for a God of love, whereas Brand's God is stern but just, like the Parson himself.

THE MAYOR

The Mayor is a local official, the lowest ranking member of the crown-appointed Norwegian executive branch. His title of lensmand is sometimes translated as Baillie or Bailiff. Since he is an appointed official, he is unlike contemporary American mayors, who are elected. His character is venal, self-seeking. His interest in the well-being of his people is prompted largely by personal reasons: it makes him more popular. His emphasis on conformity, moderation, and compromise is the direct opposite of Brand's "all or nothing."

THE DEAN

The Dean is an appointed official of the State Church, higher in authority than Brand. His position corresponds to that of an English dean, and he is roughly equivalent to a sort of assistant bishop. His title is sometimes translated as Provost. His character is much like the Mayor's, and his sense religion is no better developed. To both, in fact, religion is a matter for Sundays and should not be allowed to interfere with everyday life. Both subordinate religion to the welfare of the state.

EINAR

Einar is another foil (contrasting character) to Brand. His zest and joy in life in the first act afford as much contrast to Brand as his smug complacency after his conversion. His sense of religion, although much deeper than the Dean's, still lacks true sincerity.

MINOR CHARACTERS

Gerd

A young gipsy girl, half-witted but capable of perceptions lost on all but Brand. She views the little church by the fjord as ugly, and prefers her own Ice Church far in the hills. Brand's Mother is a loveless and lonely old woman, whose values, like the Mayor's, are almost entirely commercial. The Sexton and The Schoolmaster are typical of Ibsen's portrayal of minor officials, for they are far more concerned with keeping their own positions than with any higher issues. The Doctor, like most Ibsen's doctors, is a wise man, and his sayings must be considered carefully.

PEER GYNT

INTRODUCTION

Most critics agree that *Peer Gynt* is the opposite of *Brand*, just as the extreme idealist is the exact opposite of the clever opportunist. But the two plays have some things in common. In *Brand*, through the tragedy of an idealist, Ibsen strikes out against spiritual indifference, while in *Peer Gynt* he attacks the same vice by portraying the spiritual laxness of a self-seeker.

The great attraction that the play had in Ibsen's times as it has in our own is its lyrical freshness and beauty. The verse is, if anything, more melodious than that of *Brand*, and the subject matter, drawn in part from Norwegian folk tales, has all of the attractiveness of that type of literature. In fact many of the scenes are derived from a group of tales. "Reindeer Hunting in the Ronde Hills," in an 1848 Dano-Norwegian collection of Norwegian tales. The reindeer ride (I, i), the Saeter-girls, or cowherd girls (II, iii), and the Boyg (II, vii) are all from this source. Also inspired by this collection are the Green-Clad One (III, iii), parts of the hill-troll **episode** (II, vi), and the thread-ball scene (V, vi).

Peer Gynt was written in southern Italy in 1867, and published in November of that year. It proved popular, but not so much as *Brand*, only two more editions appearing in the next seven years. Like *Brand*, it needed considerable abridgment for the stage. The first performance was in 1876 at Christiania (now Oslo), with the famous incidental music by Edvard Grieg.

The play deals with an imaginative, indolent, self-seeking son of a spendthrift father. Peer is famous as a storyteller, only he always makes himself the hero of the stories, claiming for himself the deeds of folk heroes long ago, such as riding a reindeer over a cliff (I, i). Throughout most of the play he seeks only to please and to enrich himself. He follows the Troll King's advice - "To yourself, be enough" - far different from Brand's demand of the ideal, "all or nothing." The quest to be enough to himself leads Peer eventually to become extremely wealthy, only to lose most of his money before he returns. Then he undergoes a sort of reclamation of character in which he gradually is able to take a more serious view of himself and his limitations. *Peer Gynt*, then, is the comedy, with serious overtones, of a man without moral stability.

CHARACTERS

ASE (pronounced Osa), widow of Jon Gynt, a wealthy but spendthrift peasant.

Peer Gynt (pronounced Pair Gunt), her son.

Aslak, a blacksmith.

A Stranger and his Wife.

Solveig and Helga, their daughters.

The Owner Of Haegstad Farm. Ingrid, his daughter.

The Bridegroom and his Parents.

Three Saeter-Girls or Cowherd Girls (a saeter is a mountain hut).

A Woman In Green.

The Troll King, her father. See note below.

Kari, a Cottager's wife.

Monsieur Ballon, Herr Von Eberkopf, Mr. Cotton, Herr Trumpeterstraale, tourists.

Anitra, daughter of a Sheik.

Professor Begriffenfeldt, director of Lunatic Asylum at Cairo.

Huhu, a language reformer from Malabar.

Hussein, a Near-Eastern Secretary of State.

A Norwegian Sea Captain.

A Strange Passenger.

A Button-Molder.

A Thin Man.

Note

In Scandinavian folklore, trolls are sometimes giants, like the Boyg, but usually dwarfs. As dwarfs they are generally friendly but nearly always mischievous.

PEER GYNT

TEXTUAL ANALYSIS

ACT ONE

ACT ONE, SCENE ONE

Act One, Scene One (the Gynts' ramshackle farm). *Peer Gynt* has just returned, empty-handed and without his gun, from a hunting trip. He invents a story to explain his mishaps, telling his mother Ase how he shot a reindeer and jumped upon it to finish the kill when the beast leaped up and carried him on its back along a mountain ridge and over a cliff into a lake. Ase is very much concerned, until she remembers having heard the same story years before. She reviles Peer as a liar and a teller of wild tales, and bemoans his loss of the Haegstad farmer's daughter Ingrid, with whose dowry the Gynts could once more be wealthy as they were in the days before Jon Gynt, Peer's father, spent all his money. Ingrid is to marry the village idiot on the next day, so Peer goes off to the wedding to see what he can do, first putting his mother on the roof of a nearby mill so that she cannot follow. But Ase is let down by some neighbors and immediately sets out in pursuit.

Comment

The **exposition** (that is, disclosure of basic facts) is neatly handled in this first scene through the stories of Peer, who thus shows himself a first-rate storyteller as well as a good-for-nothing, and through the heated arguments between him and Ase. From these we learn of the past wealth of the Gynts, of their present poverty, and how Peer will do nothing to help.

ACT ONE, SCENE TWO

Act One, Scene Two (a little hill by the road near Haegstad). Peer is now reluctant to continue, conscious of his own rags and of the jeers he usually gets in company. To compensate, he lies down and looks at the clouds, dreaming of himself as Emperor, with a thousand followers. At this moment Aslak the smith walks by, who soundly thrashed Peer six weeks ago. Aslak taunts Peer, suggesting that Ingrid was once fond of him. Despite these taunts, and his ragged condition, Peer sees the dancing and the girls at the farm below and goes off to the party.

Comment

Peer's insecurity is clear: he resents and even fears the way people talk about him. He loses himself in a day dream for a while, only to be brought back sharply to reality by the smith's taunts. Finally he becomes almost intoxicated by the sound and sight of dancing, enough to conquer his fear and shame.

ACT ONE, SCENE THREE

Act One, Scene Three (the farm at Haegstad). Peer meets a frosty reception: no one, man or girl, will talk to him, except Aslak and a few of his friends who jeer at him. Peer tells tales, and the more he tells, the more he is laughed at. Aslak determines to thrash Peer, but Ase enters ready to fight in defense of her son. Suddenly the bridegroom points to the hillside, and there far above, Peer is carrying off the bride Ingrid.

Comment

In this act, we clearly see the contempt most of his neighbors have for Peer, the drunkard, storyteller, and ne'er-do-well. But Peer finally does something besides talking when he triumphantly carries off the bride. The character of Ase comes through particularly well, when she detests what Peer has done yet still wants to protect him from punishment. It is important also that only one girl of all the wedding guests will talk to Peer-Solveig, the daughter of a stranger. The young golden-haired girl makes a great impression on Peer, as the first scene of the next act discloses.

PEER GYNT

TEXTUAL ANALYSIS

ACT TWO

ACT TWO, SCENE ONE

(a narrow mountain path). Having carried Ingrid off, Peer now decides to leave her, because he loves a girl with golden hair, a white apron, and a silver-clasped prayer book (Solveig). Despite all of Ingrid's entreaties, he remains unshaken in his new-found resolve to be true to the one woman of his dreams.

ACT TWO, SCENE TWO

(a mountain lake). Ase tells Solveig about how she and Peer used to tell fairy tales together to pass the time while her husband foolishly spent all of their money. Although she is angry that Peer has done wrong, she is still happy that he has finally done something. Ase, Solveig, and her father continue looking for Peer.

ACT TWO, SCENE THREE

(bare hilltops). Fleeing from his pursuers, Peer encounters three saeter-girls (or cowherd girls), who are calling upon the trolls to spend the night with them, since their men have left them. Peer agrees to accommodate all three, and they dance off together over the hills.

ACT TWO, SCENE FOUR

(mountains). Peer enters dizzy, with an obvious hangover, dreaming of palaces and of the former wealth of the Gynts. He expresses a desire to fly until he is "pure and clean." Finally intoxicated with thoughts of his own future greatness, he leaps forward and runs his face into a rock.

Comment

In the first scene. Peer is inflexibly resolved to be true to Solveig, whose interest in Peer becomes evident in the second scene, when she insists that Ase tell all about her son. Our hero's moral fervor does not last long. He goes off with the three girls for a night, then the next day he dreams mostly of greatness and a little of purity. His final plunge into the rock is a fine ironic comment on the disparity between man's dreams and accomplishments. But we should notice that Peer's dream of greatness, like his earlier dream of Empire, is a general vision, not anything even approaching a goal to strive for.

ACT TWO, SCENE FIVE

(a mountainside). A Woman in Green crosses the hillside, followed by Peer, prancing about ridiculously like a foolish lover. They boast of each other's parentage and wealth. The Woman, we learn, is the Troll King's daughter. Peer and the Troll Princess get along well; to each black seems white, ugly seems beautiful, and filthy appears clean. They ride off together on a huge Pig.

ACT TWO, SCENE SIX

(the broken-down Royal Hall of the Troll King). Peer proves quite adaptable to troll life. He approves wholeheartedly of the troll motto: "Troll, to yourself be enough." He eats the sour-tasting troll food without much complaint, and even agrees to wear a tail. A hideously clumsy troll dance he even concedes to be delightful. But Peer refuses to have his vision permanently changed, so that he must always see things the troll way. The Troll King insists that Peer marry his daughter, because she has been made pregnant by Peer's desire for her. Upon our hero's refusal, all of the trolls attack, and the scene closes with Peer on the floor under a huge pile of kicking and biting troll children. All of the trolls suddenly run away at the sound of church bells in the distance.

Comment

By now, no one is astonished to see Peer getting along so well with the trolls. In this respect, Peer may be intended as a satire on the social ease and grace of nineteenth-century society—the qualities we now call adaptability. The central passage in these scenes, and really the first clear statement of the theme of the play, is the troll motto. The philosopher Kierkegaard continually advised his contemporary man to be himself. The Troll King refers to this saying in the "outside world," and then gives the trolls' own version. The "enough" is the key word, for it is the exact opposite of what Brand asks of man. To follow the Troll King's advice is easy. All one has to do is to satisfy oneself, that is, do enough for oneself. This rule embodies a self-seeking and intensely selfish philosophy-one we have already seen at work in Peer's lazy self-indulgence. He does not really need the Troll King's advice, for he has been living troll-style all his life.

ACT TWO, SCENE SEVEN

(darkness). Peer encounters a formless monster, the great Boyg, which blocks his every attempt to pass. The Boyg tells Peer to go roundabout. Our hero can neither kill nor injure the monster, which is finally eliminated by the sound of church bells.

Comment

The Boyg's advice, like the Troll King's, is the exact opposite of what Brand would have one do. The advice to go roundabout is a perfect complement to a rule of life that emphasizes simply to do enough for oneself. The Boyg itself is a mythical troll monster, dispersed, like the trolls, at the sound of church bells.

ACT TWO, SCENE EIGHT

(a hut on a hillside). In this very short scene, Peer sees Solveig, who runs away. He gives her little sister a silver button to speak in his behalf to Solveig.

Comment

This brief scene is a good example of roundabout action. Rather than pursue Solveig by himself, Peer takes an easier course.

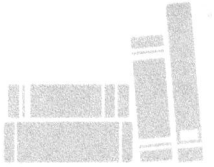

PEER GYNT

TEXTUAL ANALYSIS

ACT THREE

ACT THREE, SCENE ONE

Act Three, Scene One (a pine wood.) While cutting down trees to build a cabin, Peer dreams of a big house with a tower and a weather vane, then decides to settle for a small thatched hut. He observes a young man cut off his finger to avoid being drafted into the army. The deed impresses him: "The thought, perhaps the desire, the will - these I can understand - but really to do the deed!"

Comment

Although Peer's remark refers to the young man's self-mutilation, it also has an application to his own life, since Peer has so far shown himself able to think and to wish, but not very able to do things. The young man will be the subject of a funeral sermon in Act Five, scene three.

ACT THREE, SCENE TWO

Act Three, Scene Two (Ase's house). Ase and her neighbor Kari go through what little has been left after the legal settlement taken by the Haegstad farmer for the abduction of Ingrid. But the devoted Ase still tries to mend shirts and socks for her darling boy.

ACT THREE, SCENE THREE

Act Three, Scene Three (a forest hut). Peer Gynt and Solveig will set up house in his new hut. But an ancient woman in green approaches with an ugly brat by her side - the Troll Princess and the child of Peer's desires. She promises to harass him constantly if he marries Solveig. Faced with a decision, he decides against the straight road of repentance in favor of the roundabout course of flight.

Comment: Peer justifies his cowardly choice by voicing platitudes on how it would be sacrilege to meet Solveig as he now is.

ACT THREE, SCENE FOUR

Act Three, Scene Four (Ase's room). Peer visits his dying mother, and they make believe he is driving her off in a sleigh to a feast in a far-off castle. She dies, and Peer then departs for the coast.

Comment

Peer shows his great love for his mother in this scene, as she does for him. It is significant that her life should end with the same sort of fairy tale with which she and her son spent so many of their earlier years.

PEER GYNT

TEXTUAL ANALYSIS

ACT FOUR

ACT FOUR, SCENES ONE AND TWO

Act Four, Scenes One And Two (the Moroccan coast). Peer discourses with four yachting acquaintances on how he became wealthy by trading in slaves for America and idols and missionaries for China. In a fit of rhapsody, he describes the "Gyntian Self" as made up of wishes, appetites, desires, fancies, claims, and aspirations. Now middle-aged, he still entertains his old ambition to become an emperor. Although they show themselves to be scoundrels, the four tourist friends are duly shocked when Peer tells them that he intends to help the Turks against the Greeks. They run off with the ship, which promptly explodes with the loss of the whole crew and all of Peer's treasure. The rascally Peer commends himself to God: "The Lord will provide."

ACT FOUR, SCENES THREE AND FOUR

Act Four, Scenes Three And Four (a grove). Peer is now fighting off the attacks of a crowd of apes, complaining that "his Creator's image" must so suffer.

ACT FOUR, SCENE FIVE

Act Four, Scene Five (a desert cave). Peer comes walking along, spouting scraps of Scripture, and dreaming of plans to reclaim the desert. He sees the Emperor's horse and robes which a group of thieves had left, and dresses himself and gallops off.

ACT FOUR, SCENES SIX, SEVEN, EIGHT

Act Four, Scenes Six, Seven, Eight (a desert, at or near an oasis). Peer finds solace in the arms of the desert beauty Anitra, even if she is a little fat and very dirty. While the middle-aged Peer makes foolish love to her, she strips him of his jewels and money and then gallops off.

ACT FOUR, SCENE NINE

Act Four, Scene Nine (the same oasis). Disappointed in love, Peer resolves to devote his life to the study of history. He is so affected by his determination that he cannot hold back a tear, especially since through history he will become Manhood's Emperor.

Comment

So far in this act, Peer has been living a good troll life making money, gratifying himself, spending money, and always aspiring to become greater: that is, to make more money. Throughout all this time he continues to maintain a very respectable front by constantly uttering bits of the Bible here and empty moral-sounding phrases there. Occasionally these are a good source of comedy, as when he looks out at his sinking ship and exclaims: "He [the Lord] takes a fatherly interest in my welfare, but He's not very economical about it." The total impression we get of Peer is not very favorable, although he always appears typically human, especially in the scenes with Anitra, where he is a tired and foolish man of wealth being cheated of his money.

ACT FOUR, SCENE TEN

Act Four, Scene Ten (a forest in Norway). Solveig sings her song of patient waiting for Peer.

ACT FOUR, SCENES ELEVEN, TWELVE, THIRTEEN

Act Four, Scenes Eleven, Twelve, Thirteen (Memnon's statue, Sphinx, Insane Asylum at Cairo). Peer observes the statue of Memnon, then the Sphinx, which he identifies with the Boyg. He is then taken off to the Insane Asylum at Cairo by its director, Professor Begriffenfeldt. Here he encounters a language reformer, a man who thinks he is a pen, and another who imagines himself a king. Peer faints and is crowned "Emperor of Self."

> Comment

Solveig's patient waiting prepares the reader and audience for her acceptance of Peer at the end of the play. Peer's wandering course through this act could not end more appropriately than in an insane asylum. His coronation as "Emperor of Self" is an ironic comment on his very lack of self, on his shallowness and superficiality of character.

PEER GYNT

TEXTUAL ANALYSIS

ACT FIVE

....

ACT FIVE, SCENE ONE

Act Five, Scene One (a ship on the North Sea). Now an old man, Peer discusses homecoming with the ship's captain and resolves to give each sailor some little present, until he learns that even the meanest of the sailors has a wife and family and the comforts of home, however poor, waiting for him. In a fit of jealous rage, Peer vows to give the crew nothing except perhaps some liquor to make them drunk enough to forget their families. Peer then becomes indignant when the captain refuses because of the very rough sea to rescue three survivors of a wrecked small craft. He complains that there is no more faith in Christianity left among men.

Our hero is then accosted by a strange passenger who suggests that if Peer were to die, he should leave his body for the stranger, who is interested in examining men's dreams and capacity for them. Peer dismisses him as a blasphemous freethinker. The ship strikes a reef and sinks.

ACT FIVE, SCENE TWO

Act Five, Scene Two (a small boat). Peer fights the cook for possession of the overturned lifeboat, first allowing him a little time to pray before drowning. The strange passenger swims by, again asking for Peer's corpse, chats with him about terror and victory gained through terror, and then disappears.

Comment

The inconsistency of Peer comes across well in these scenes. He maintains a veneer of respectability, mouthing all of the appropriate Christian sentiments, yet his determination to leave the whole crew intoxicated is not due to any Christian motive. What Peer is, many people in the nineteenth century were: moral hypocrites, speaking fair sentiments, but acting selfishly. Although Ibsen had his own contemporary Norwegians in mind, the satiric effect of such passages as these is general, for the entire human race suffers from Peer's faults.

The appearance of the strange passenger calls for some explanation. That only Peer sees him makes his other-worldly nature obvious. Our hero's reaction to him, calling him blasphemous, is characteristic of his outward respectability. The true nature of the stranger seems to be disclosed in the second scene, in his discussion of terror or fear, which, in Kierkegaard's system of thought, here probably has reference to a terrifying conviction of guilt for sin. Thus the stranger may be regarded as a reflection of Peer's own conscience. The stranger's insistence on examining Peer's body to study dreams suggests a developing insecurity within Peer which he still denies on the surface.

ACT FIVE, SCENE THREE

Act Five, Scene Three (churchyard in the mountains). Peer listens to a priest's long sermon on the industrious and useful life led by a man who, having maimed himself by cutting off a finger to avoid military service (III, i), ever afterwards works hard and supports a wife and three sons until the day of his death. The priest insists that his insignificant man was great, because he was himself. The message is lost on Peer, who comments on the comfort of the sermon and the beautiful Christian custom of praising the dead.

ACT FIVE, SCENE FOUR

Act Five, Scene Four (the ruins of the Gynt estate). Peer Gynt sees an auction of the remains of his estate. He offers for sale a castle, a horse, a vision of a silver-clasped prayer book (Solveig's in II, i), a crown of straw, and the Prophet's beard. His conduct excites the official interest of the Mayor, but Peer concludes by telling a story of the devil, who presented an imitation of a pig's squeal by hiding a pig in his costume. All of the spectators felt that the devil's performance was exaggerated. Peer draws the moral that the devil was stupid for not taking the measure of his audience first.

Comment

The churchyard scene recalls the earlier scene (III, i), when Peer watched the youth cut off his finger and marveled at the latter's ability to perform the action as well as just wish to. That the youth afterward found himself is clear, just as it is equally evident that Peer has not yet found himself. The "Gyntian Self" he boasted about earlier (IV, i) is only his outward self, his veneer.

The next scene is important, for it shows Peer first of all auctioning off his former life in symbols - the prayer book, castle, crown, etc. The concluding tale has a double-edged moral, for as the Devil misjudged his audience, Peer misjudged his.

ACT FIVE, SCENE FIVE

Act Five, Scene Five (before Solveig's hut). Peer is picking and eating wild onions. He compares himself to one, then peels it layer by layer, each layer representing one of his former careers. There is no kernel, only layers. He recognizes the hut, then Solveig's voice. Suddenly he perceives the truth: "Oh dread! Here lay my Empire!" But he runs off into the woods.

Comment: Peer is finally coming to a more serious view of himself, to a realization that his life has been literally frittered away. The comparison of himself to an onion is apt, since as one "Gyntian Self" (see IV, i) after another is peeled away, the remainder is nothing; for Peer has never developed a self, his own self. His comment "Oh dread!" is important, since the word (angst in the original) in Kierkegaardian thought refers to a terrible conviction of guilt. Despite his soul-searching, he still follows the Boyg's advice, going roundabout by running away.

ACT FIVE, SCENE SIX

Act Five, Scene Six (a field laid waste by a forest fire). Running across the field, Peer stumbles over thread-balls, which proclaim themselves thoughts that he should have had. The leaves are watchwords he would have spoken had it not been for his laziness. The sighing of the breeze becomes songs he never sang. Dewdrops are tears he never shed, and broken straws are deeds he never did. Finally Ase's voice accuses him of having driven her the wrong way (see III, iv).

ACT FIVE SCENE SEVEN

Act Five Scene Seven (the same). Peer meets a button-molder, whose task is to melt down and recast the souls of people who have been neither great sinners nor very virtuous. Peer objects, and is given a little more time, until they meet again at the next crossroads.

Comment

The symbolism of the thread-balls, leaves, etc., in the sixth scene is obvious. The button-molder, however, needs some explanation. The way for his appearance has been prepared by references to Peer's casting buttons as a child (III, ii; V, iv). The button-molder serves as an agent of judgment, and as such he finds Peer wanting. The latter is judged guilty of "halvhet," literally "half-ness," which means that he failed to be anyone or anything entirely. Peer has gone through life doing enough and no more; hence he has done most things at best by halves. He has catered to his "Gyntian Self" (his desires, whims, and fancies) but he has never realized his own potential.

ACT FIVE, SCENE EIGHT

Act Five, Scene Eight (the same). Peer meets the Troll King, now an aged man abandoned by his own family. Our hero asks for character references to present to the button-molder, requesting that the Troll King state that Peer never gave in to the trolls' temptations. But the Troll King is indignant, since Peer became a very wealthy gentleman just by following the troll motto, "to yourself, be enough."

ACT FIVE, SCENE NINE

Act Five, Scene Nine (a crossroads). The button-molder accosts Peer again, and in answer to his inquiry, tells him what it means to be oneself: "To be oneself is to slay oneself ... to stand forth everywhere with the intention of the Master fully displayed." Peer gets a stay of execution until the next crossroads.

Comment: The Troll King arrives at an opportune time to give Peer a chance to realize the futility of the troll motto, "enough." An important minor source of comedy in this scene, as in II, vi, is the extreme nationalism of the Troll King, whereby Ibsen satirizes the burgeoning nationalistic movement in Norway.

The words of the button-molder are enigmatic. His statement, "To be oneself is to slay oneself," suggests that to be oneself, that is to realize what God the Master intends one to be, one must slay his "Gyntian Self," that is, his superficial desires and fancies. Peer has failed to do this, for he has developed only the "Gyntian Self" (see V, v).

ACT FIVE, SCENE TEN

Act Five, Scene Ten (a grassy hillside). Peer sees a thin man in a priest's clothing and asks him for advice. The priest, however, wears a cloven hoof. Undaunted, Peer asks him for refuge, but is refused on the grounds that his sins are not important. He has not done enough either to rejoice or to fear, only enough to fret about. The thin man goes on to explain how some people make of themselves only a negative picture of what they were intended to be. He is looking for one such negative person, Peer Gynt. Our hero promptly directs the priest-devil to Cape of Good Hope, and then walks off meditating on his loneliness and insignificance. He designs an **epitaph** for his tomb: "Here no one lies buried."

ACT FIVE, SCENE ELEVEN

Act Five, Scene Eleven (a crossroads near a mountain hut). The button-molder again accosts Peer, but lets him go until the third crossroads. Peer hears Solveig singing, approaches the hut, remembers the Boyg's advice to "go roundabout," but decides at last to go straight ahead. He asks Solveig a riddle: 'where has the true Peer Gynt been since they parted?' Solveig's answer surprises him: 'In my faith, my hope, and my love.'" Peer finally realizes that in Solveig he has been turning away the love of both a mother and a wife. She folds him in her arms as the drama ends.

Comment

The devil, in the shape of the thin man, again repeats the **theme** of "half-ness." Peer's sins are not important enough for him to be damned, since his life has been a half-hearted following of self-interest, bolstered lip-service to conventional morality. Peer finally realizes his own shortcomings when he composes the **epitaph** for his grave.

In the last scene, we see that Peer is finally saved not so much by his own action as by Solveig's love. That her love is now a maternal love is appropriate not only for their advanced age, but even more because the one person Peer really seemed to love besides his vision of Solveig was his mother. By accepting Solveig's love, and no longer running away from his own feelings for her, Peer has finally come to an acceptance of self and of life.

PEER GYNT

CHARACTER ANALYSES

PEER GYNT

Peer Gynt is a shallow, self-seeking opportunist, a romantic teller of tales. He is the personification of the quality of joy of life, but he is also made very human, especially in his ability to justify all his actions as Christian. At one point (V, iii) he even refers to himself as "poor but still virtuous." He is much more human than the driving reformer Brand, simply because he is much more fallible. He develops in the course of the play from a wild, carefree youth, through a complacent, callous, amorous, and sometimes foolish middle age, to a hard-bitten yet finally repentant old age.

ASE

Ase, his mother, is equally fond of fairy tales, but at the same time she has a sense of responsibility to herself, her son, and the community that Peer completely lacks. Her love for her son, however, always triumphs over her dislike of his lazy and irresponsible ways. Although she would often like to see him punished for his misdeeds, she will allow no one to chastise him but herself.

SOLVEIG

Solveig is at the beginning of the play a young girl with flowing blond hair, clinging to her mother's skirt. She matures rapidly into a woman willing to give up all to wait for her loved one, Peer. She finally becomes a maternal old lady overflowing with love for the errant Peer.

A DOLL'S HOUSE

INTRODUCTION

Written in prose, and considerably shorter than *Brand* and *Peer Gynt*, *A Doll's House* is the second of Ibsen's great realistic social dramas. The play deals with the issue of the position of woman in marriage and in society. In Ibsen's day, the following opinions of marriage were prevalent:

1. In the business of the home, the wife was more of a servant than a helper.

2. She could influence home policies and decisions-only indirectly by suggestions to her husband.

3. She was expected to look up to her husband as an Ideal-Maker.

4. She was to follow the lead of her husband: "I will be your conscience and your will."

5. She would therefore become a somewhat useful but very decorative member of the household, to be loved and

cherished by her husband, but not to share in any family responsibilities or troubles.

In such a system of marriage, the frivolity, romanticizing, and occasional lying that characterize Nora are to be expected. Unable by social **convention** to have a truly deep and serious share in the marriage, the wife must rely on either escapist dreams or petty subterfuges to adjust to her situation.

Although the play has a serious **theme** and deals with what was in Ibsen's day a topic of great concern, woman's rights, it is essentially a comedy rather than a tragedy. Ibsen maintains the comic spirit by his subtle characterization of Nora as a romantic dreamer whose grasp on reality is conditioned by her dreams, ideals, and wishes, and of Torvald, her husband, whose pose of strict high-minded morality nearly always crumbles into petty selfishness when he is faced by a crisis.

The play proved successful both on the stage and in print, but Ibsen was compelled soon after its first performance in 1879 to write an alternate conclusion in which Nora returns to her husband. With this happy ending, the play was shortly produced in nearly every European country, with considerable acclaim, and much heated discussion of the problems raised.

CHARACTERS

Torvald Helmer, a lawyer and a newly appointed bank manager.

Nora, his wife.

Doctor Rank, a family friend.

Mrs. Christina Linde, a widow.

Nils Krogstad, a former lawyer, now a small-time journalist and minor employee of Torvald's bank.

The Three Helmer Children; Anne, their nurse; A Housemaid; A Porter.

The setting is the tastefully furnished home of the Helmers. The time: Act One, Christmas Eve; Act Two, Christmas Day; Act Three, the next night.

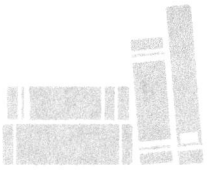

A DOLL'S HOUSE

TEXTUAL ANALYSIS

ACT ONE

The doorbell rings and Nora enters, happily humming a tune, followed by a porter with a Christmas tree. She removes her coat and hat, quickly snatching a couple of macaroons from her pocket and eating them. She listens at her husband's door, and he greets her as his "little lark," and "little squirrel." Torvald teases her about her extravagance, then asks her what she would like for Christmas. She would prefer money, thus provoking a further good-natured lesson on spendthrifts and secret macaroon eaters. Torvald sees her improvidence with money as inherited from her father.

The doorbell rings, and Mrs. Christina Linde is ushered in. At first Nora does not recognize her friend of ten years before, since the latter has changed so much. Nora then tells of her happy life with Torvald and their three children for the last eight years, while Christina speaks of how her deceased husband left her nothing. Nora tells Christina how she got money from her father to take Torvald to Italy for a year when his health was so bad that he was in danger of death. Christina hopes Torvald can find work of her. Nora is confident he will.

Nora then discloses how she borrowed the money for their trip to Italy and has been struggling to pay it back ever since. To Nora, the whole matter is a secret which she jealously guards from her husband. Nora is so romantically simple about the loan that she is ignorant even of how much she has so far paid in interest and principal.

Doctor Rank enters and mentions that the "morally sick" Nils Krogstad is at present with Torvald. Nora is happy to learn that Krogstad is now an employee of her husband, since thus Torvald has power over him. Doctor Rank sees her with the forbidden macaroons, but she says Christina brought them.

Nora then plays hide and seek with her children, until Krogstad appears. He demands that Nora use her influence with her husband on his behalf, since he is afraid of losing his position. Krogstad threatens to tell Torvald that she borrowed money from him on a note or bond with a forged signature. Nora's reaction is one of indignation, for the loan is her secret. Krogstad then produces evidence of her forgery of her father's signature on the original loan papers.

Nora freely admits it, but sees no harm in what she did. He leaves, threatening to expose her if he loses his job. Nora is plainly worried. She intercedes with Torvald for Krogstad, but to no avail. Torvald tells her of Krogstad's past misdeed, a forgery, and he then lectures her on the wickedness of committing evil and evading punishment. He states that nearly everyone who has turned bad early in life had a lying mother. Frightened by what she has heard, Nora refuses to see her children for fear of poisoning their minds.

Comment

For his basic **exposition** or disclosure of essential facts, Ibsen uses the device of having Nora talk about her last eight years to Christina. The complexity of Nora's character is evident. At first glance, she seems two separate persons, one a frivolous but obedient and submissive wife, the other a surprisingly resourceful little schemer. A more careful study shows that the two faces of Nora are really one very human but very complicated personality. The key to an understanding of Nora is her obsessive lying. She lies about the macaroons to Torvald and later to Dr. Rank. She tells her husband that Christina came especially to see him. Her lies are small lies, but they are indicative of the great lie that Nora must constantly live. To measure up to the contemporary ideal of what a wife should be, she must always idolize her husband, and spend her time as his "little squirrel," playing with the children. Her habit of lying is a partly subconscious way of fighting back against this repressive environment. Her chief compensation for this environment, however, is her secret, a source of continual joy and comfort to her. Thus Nora is living a lie: she appears to her husband a rather flighty, irresponsible yet thoroughly lovable little creature, while all the time she has been trying to pay off the large debt she contracted when she saved Torvald's life by getting them all a much needed vacation in Italy.

Nora's relation with Krogstad also shows the same complexity of character. Apart from her own two worlds-her husband and children on the one hand and her secret on the other-she is not interested. She detests Krogstad for his annoying insistence that she get her father to countersign the loan, not considering or realizing that even in this way the transaction was irregular since a wife could not borrow money without her husband's consent. The scene in which Krogstad finally wrings a confession from her is particularly illuminating. She insists that the signature is her father's until faced by clear evidence, then blandly admits that she signed it. She lies and evades the issues until finally confronted by the evidence. After this admission she continues to look upon her deed as a brave act of love, and refuses to consider the possibility of technical guilt. Nora's reactions here suggest her essential ability to romance, to imagine the world a little different from the way it really is, for the comfort of herself and her loved ones.

A DOLL'S HOUSE

TEXTUAL ANALYSIS

ACT TWO

The Christmas tree has already been stripped of its ornaments. Nora is anxious about the possibility of a letter from Krogstad to Torvald. Contemplating suicide, she asks the nurse how her children would be if she were to go away for good. She tries to busy herself with preparations for the next day's costume ball, but she cannot bury her fear of discovery.

Christina enters and she recommends that Nora see a little less of their family friend, Doctor Rank, because his frequent visits seem a little suspicious. She suspects that Nora may have borrowed the money from the doctor, but Nora denies it. Christina asks for a showdown on the matter of the loan since it is bothering Nora so much, but Torvald comes in just as she begins her questioning.

Nora begs her husband not to dismiss Krogstad, but Torvald has already made up his mind to fire him, not for morals or for any lack of ability, but because Torvald cannot bear the way Krogstad speaks to him familiarly just because they used to be playmates years before. Nora considers her husband's reason narrow-minded, thus provoking him into sending a letter of dismissal to Krogstad immediately. Nora is afraid of possible consequences, but Torvald boasts that he will take them all upon himself. Nora answers that he will never have to.

Doctor Rank comes in to tell Nora that his inherited disease has finally taken its toll, and he will be dead within the month. He promises to send his card with a black cross on it as soon as his "loathsome end has started." Nora is about to ask him for a favor, probably about her trouble with Krogstad, when he discloses his love for her. Nora is rather disappointed and uneasy, for their relationship was so simple before. Now she feels unable to ask for his help. Their conversation is cut short by the arrival of Krogstad who waits for her in the kitchen.

Krogstad warns Nora against running away or committing suicide, because he lacked the courage for such desperate measures after he had been detected in forgery. He tells Nora that he intends to use her bond or loan-agreement as a lever to gain a higher position at the bank and then take control of the establishment away from Torvald. He drops a letter explaining all to Torvald into the mailbox and leaves.

Christina enters, sees Nora agitated about the letter, and suspects Krogstad. Nora admits it, and also her forgery. Christina goes off to see what she can do, since formerly she knew Krogstad very well.

Torvald goes to the letter box, but is stopped by Nora, who wants him to rehearse her dancing of the tarantella. She dances frantically, her hair falling over her shoulders. Torvald promises to forget about business and letters and devote his time to her until after the dance.

Comment

In this act, Torvald's true character begins to unfold. At first he appears an extremely upright, moral individual, so fastidious in his morals that evil, like Krogstad's forgery, makes him ill. When we hear his motives for firing the disreputable bank clerk, they are not moral at all, but based only on his own personal embarrassment at being addressed by an inferior with the familiar Du in Dano-Norwegian. Torvald is Nora's ideal, but here she sees only narrow-mindedness. But when he says he will take all of the consequences of firing Krogstad on his own shoulders, the romanticizing Nora reinterprets his boast as an assurance that he would, if the truth were known, take the blame for her misdeed. This interpretation soon becomes a conviction, so that Nora hopes for yet prays against such a possibility.

Nora's reactions in the scene with Doctor Rank seem inconsistent. To save Torvald's honor and her own, she has determined to ask him for an unspecified favor. She is so wound up in her own troubles that she interprets his veiled comments on death as dealing with her own dreams of suicide. When he finally states that he is near death Nora seems relieved rather than concerned. She is so involved with her own problems that she has no time for or patience with his. Her reaction to his avowal of love is along the same lines. She was looking for a heroic gesture of assistance from the Doctor, but before they can get that far he makes a rather meek protestation of love. As far as Nora is concerned, the whole scene is ruined; hence she shows her extreme displeasure and cannot bring herself to ask any favors of him.

Nora's frantic dancing at the end of the act expresses her almost hysterical tension. She dances to put off what at the moment seems inevitable, her death. As she put it, "Seven hours to midnight, then twenty-four hours to the next midnight. Then the tarantella will be over... Thirty-one hours to live."

A DOLL'S HOUSE

TEXTUAL ANALYSIS

ACT THREE

Christina speaks to Krogstad of their past lives, how she jilted him to marry for money to support her mother and brothers, and now has nothing to show for it. Now that she has his job at the bank, she suggests that they join forces. She as much as proposes to him. He offers to ask Torvald for the letter back again but Christina prefers that the truth be disclosed, come what may. Krogstad leaves, but will return later to see her home.

Nora and Torvald come in, the latter flushed with excitement and champagne. Christina recommends that Nora tell him all, but she cannot. After Christina leaves, Torvald, inspired by the tarantella and the champagne, becomes a little romantic, only to have the arrival of Doctor Rank rescue the unsympathetic and rather cold Nora. The Doctor jokes morbidly about his being invisible at the next ball, then takes what is to be his final leave.

Torvald opens the letter box and first sees Doctor Rank's calling card with the black cross. They briefly discuss his death, then Torvald, in a romantic fervor, wishes that Nora might face some great danger so that he could risk his life and everything for her sake. Nora simply asks him to read his mail, then she is about to rush out of the house when Torvald returns with Krogstad's letter. Her first few answers to his expostulations suggest that she still hoped he would at least offer to take the responsibility upon himself. First she says that she loved him above everything else; second, that Torvald should not suffer for her sake and should not take the blame himself. All he can do is to accuse her and revile her for her wickedness. The nearest he can come to the heroic generosity Nora was hoping for is to allow her to remain in the house, although not as a wife and not with the children. Happiness is nothing to him compared with saving appearances.

The arrival of a second letter from Krogstad, in which he announces his intention of pursuing the matter no further, brings a sudden change in Torvald. He insists that Nora forget all that he said while he was overwhelmed by the probability of ruin, and he claims to have forgiven her completely. He delivers a long lecture on womanly helplessness and the masculine virtue of forgiveness. Nora is unimpressed.

Nora makes Torvald sit down for a serious talk. She tells him the facts of their marriage. This is the first serious talk they have had since they first knew one another. First her father, then Torvald have treated her like a doll to be kind to and play with, but not to take seriously or to talk to about serious things. She declares her intention of leaving him in order to educate herself. She tells Torvald she no longer loves him because he is not the man she thought he was, since a short while before he could not rise to any heroism in her behalf. When Torvald answers that "no man would sacrifice his honor for the woman he loves," Nora counters: "It's something hundreds of thousands of women have done." Nora will leave immediately, because she "cannot spend the night under a stranger's roof." They return each other's wedding rings, and as she leaves, she gives Torvald one last hope. She will return only if a "wonderful thing" happens. The play ends with the sound of the street door shutting below.

Comment

Krogstad's sudden conversion from villain to hero seems inadequately motivated, although Ibsen tries to make it appear reasonable by informing us of an earlier love affair between the former lawyer and Christina.

The scene in which Torvald learns Nora's secret from the letter is revealing of both characters. Torvald is seen in his true light as an insufferably strict moralist stripped of his moral exterior and reduced to considering only the appearance of things. The punishment he lays out for Nora is typical of the man's hypocrisy. Outwardly, things will appear the same, but Nora will no longer be allowed to be a wife to him or a mother to the children. But as soon as he reads the second letter, he becomes his usual moralizing, high-sounding self again.

Led to expect better things of her husband by his empty boast of risking all for her, and by her own romantic dreams of a miracle, Nora is thoroughly disappointed by his petty conduct. Far from being much of a hero, Torvald does not even strike her as much of a man.

Nora's capacity for self-dramatization, so obvious in the tarantella scene at the end of Act Two, is given its fullest play in the final great scene between herself and Torvald. Particularly theatrical is her declaration that she cannot live another night under a strange man's roof. Ibsen has often been criticized for making this scene a little too melodramatic, but Nora's love for romanticizing and dramatizing is sufficient justification for her manner. Nora has been playacting most of her life, acting the part of a song-bird or squirrel-wife so well that it is hard to distinguish the acting from the real thing. When she labored to pay off her debt and keep her secret, she was playacting the part of a man and a man's responsibilities. Somehow, considering her character, we get the impression that she may be playacting now. However, she might carry on the act for three days or thirty years. Ibsen in his regular version gives us no real clue as to what might have happened after the final curtain, but he did write an alternate ending for his shocked contemporaries in which Nora returns. The character of Nora is such that she might grow tired of her new life soon, or might romanticize her way for years as an emancipated woman. The play ends with another of her romantic ideas, where she tells Torvald there may be hope of reconciliation if a "wonderful thing" happens; in other words, if they are both able to accept each other for what they are.

A DOLL'S HOUSE

CHARACTER ANALYSES

NORA

Nora is one of Ibsen's most complex female characters. She lives up to the nineteenth-century ideal of the submissive dutiful wife, yet at the same time she is resourceful in scheming to keep her secret. There is a certain amount of heroism in the way she sacrifices herself rather than her family to meet her debt. At the same time, she boasts of that heroism to Christina. She realizes that Torvald's strict ideas of morality give her no choice but to keep her secret, yet she romanticizes that secret into something that is hers and hers alone. Her childishness in handling money is not feigned, but she feigns a little more extravagance to get additional money from Torvald to meet her payments. One of the most unselfish aspects of Nora is her reason for borrowing in the first place, to save Torvald's life after his physical breakdown. She never tells this to Torvald or to Krogstad, who lends her the money, but she does brag a little about it to Christina. By these little acts of boasting, her apparent unselfishness is seen as part of a larger self-centered romanticizing, whereby she builds up for herself in her dreams a strength of character she otherwise lacks.

Nora's whole life has been one of playacting. She acts the role of a frivolous, gay, unthinking but submissive nineteenth-century wife to perfection, all the while playing the deeper role of a wife sacrificing herself for her husband. Therefore when she finally leaves Torvald, there is a quality of playacting about the way she does it. Her capacity for romanticizing and dramatizing herself is with her to the end.

TORVALD

Torvald is a nineteenth-century philistine, blindly conventional and extremely narrow-minded. He maintains an appearance of complete moral respectability, even to the point of becoming ill when he is near people like Krogstad whom he considers evil. Ironically, his own wife is guilty of the same fault Krogstad committed, forgery. His reaction to Nora's guilt is not only unheroic, but actually unmanly. He shows his true colors in that he is more worried about appearances than true morality.

CHRISTINA

Christina, Mrs. Linde, is an old friend of Nora, much aged by an unhappy and unprosperous marriage. At one time in love with Krogstad, she jilted him to marry money. Her motives seemed good to her at the time, to help her invalid mother and younger brothers, but her life seems futile now.

KROGSTAD

Krogstad is the former lawyer who lent the money to Nora for her trip. His nearly cruel persistence in seeing Nora, and especially his determination, after his dismissal, to use Nora's forged bond to gain power over Torvald, mark him as the villain of the play. His quick reclamation by Christina is forced and poorly motivated.

DOCTOR RANK

Doctor Rank is an old friend of the family, whose conversation Nora enjoys as a relief from Torvald's perpetual sermons on morality. The Doctor's love for Nora is clearly of the Platonic variety, that is, a spiritual love only. His character is a good contrast to Nora's, for his mind is active and alert, but his body is diseased as a result of his father's excesses. Nora is physically healthy, but mentally and emotionally immature as a result of first her father's, then her husband's treating her like a doll rather than a human being. The Doctor also contrasts with Torvald, who has none of Rank's charm or conversational ability. Interested only in maintaining respectability, Torvald is indifferent to art, music, or anything truly cultural, whereas Rank is well educated and able to converse on a variety of topics.

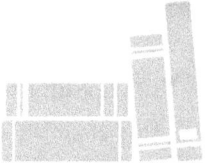

GHOSTS

INTRODUCTION

....

In this play, Ibsen presents the opposite of *A Doll's House*. Involved in an impossible marriage with a well-meaning but densely conventional husband, Nora walks out. *Ghosts*, however, is the story of a wife, Mrs. Helen Alving, who stays with a dissolute, depraved husband and receives as a reward paresis (incomplete paralysis) for her son and desperation for herself. The play deals with congenital syphilis, which is soon perceived to be a symbol for the more pervasive and dangerous "ghosts" in society, the dead, outmoded ideas and values that still cling to people and choke their lives. Ibsen is writing, then, not a medical treatise on inherited paresis, but rather a study of the effects of conventional ideas and attitudes that no longer are beneficial to society.

His contemporaries, however, could see only the taboo subject of syphilis and the possible mercy killing at the end. No other play in the century aroused such a furious reaction all over Europe. Loudest of the objectors were Ibsen's own countrymen, where even the booksellers refused to sell or stock copies of the play. Strange as it may seem, the world premiere of *Ghosts* was presented in America, the first of his plays to be produced here.

It was presented in Dano-Norwegian in several of the large cities of the Midwest in 1882. A year later the play was presented in Sweden and then in Denmark. By 1890 the play had been performed in Berlin and in Paris. The first American production in English was in 1899, for thirty-seven weeks continuously. But as late as 1906, the play was still forbidden to the public theatres in England.

Ghosts is much closer to tragedy than *A Doll's House*, in which Nora is too frivolous to make a good tragic heroine. The **protagonist** (chief character) of *Ghosts* is not the dying Oswald but rather Mrs. Alving, who is one of Ibsen's strongest and most tragic female characters.

Characters

Mrs. Helen Alving, widow of Captain Alving, who was formerly Chamberlain to the King ("Chamberlain" was an honorary title given by the king to wealthy and influential citizens).

Oswald Alving, her son, an artist.

Pastor Manders, the pastor of the parish.

Jacob Engstrand, a carpenter.

Regina Engstrand, his daughter, Mrs. Alving's maid.

The scene is Mrs. Alving's country house, near a large fjord in western Norway. The atmosphere is gloomy, and it rains steadily throughout the play.

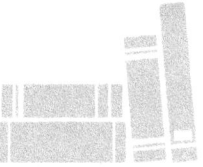

GHOSTS

TEXTUAL ANALYSIS

ACT ONE

Jacob Engstrand asks Regina to join him in a new business venture, a home for sailors. She will have nothing to do with him. From several slips that he makes, we infer that he may not really be Regina's father. Pastor Manders arrives. He and Regina discuss the return of Oswald. When the Pastor mentions Regina's father she is cold and uninterested. She leaves to summon Mrs. Alving.

The Pastor and Mrs. Alving talk about her son's homecoming. Suddenly the Pastor sees some recent books on the table and delivers her a stern lecture on reading such things. When Mrs. Alving declares her approval of them, the Pastor asks that at least she not talk about them, since one is not bound to account to everybody for what one reads and thinks at home.

Pastor Manders then discusses the establishment of the new Captain Alving Foundation, an orphanage set up with the fortune left by the late Mr. Alving. He insists that the orphanage be uninsured since many of the local people feel that insuring it would show a lack of faith. The Pastor also puts in a good word for Engstrand, who has impressed him with a sincere desire for reformation.

Oswald comes in, smoking a pipe, and the Pastor sees a resemblance between him and his late father which Mrs. Alving emphatically denies. Oswald comments on what a good and useful life his father led, and the Pastor agrees. Oswald then describes life in Paris, particularly the common-law marriages of some of his artist friends, which were quite decent and honorable despite their irregularity. The Pastor is shocked, but Mrs. Alving agrees with her son. Manders gives Mrs. Alving a sermon on marital duties and on the evil of sending her son abroad at an early age to be educated. He also particularly criticizes her for having gone to him, after she had been married a year, for refuge from her husband, and prides himself on having saved her virtue and reputation by sending her back to her husband.

Mrs. Alving then tells the Pastor that the Captain never reformed, and remained dissolute to his death. This fact she hid from everyone, including the Pastor and Oswald. Captain Alving even carried his excesses home. He was the real father of Regina, whose mother, a servant in the Alving household, was then married off in a hurry to Jacob Engstrand, with a story about an English seaman who ravished her and left her some money as reparation. Mrs. Alving emphasizes that the orphanage is built with Captain Alving's fortune so that Oswald will inherit nothing from his father. As the act closes, the Pastor and Mrs. Alving see "ghosts" from the past, for Oswald is within the dining room making overtures to a not-too-unwilling Regina.

Comment

In the first scene we get an idea of what sort of rogue Jacob Engstrand is. It becomes fairly clear that his home for sailors is not likely to be very respectable. The fact that he made a good impression on the Pastor is a tribute more to Manders' gullibility than to his own transparent duplicity.

The Pastor's true sense of values is clearly exposed in the scene with Mrs. Alving, when he condemns her reading habits without ever having read any of the books, and particularly when he cautions her above all not to talk about them. To the Pastor, it is not so much deeds or thoughts that count but appearances.

The matter of the orphanage being uninsured paves the way for its dramatic destruction by fire at the end of the second act. A further preparation is provided by Mrs. Alving's mentioning that there nearly was a small fire there recently in Engstrand's carpenter's shop. Thus the audience begins to expect a fire.

Mrs. Alving's quick denial of the resemblance between Oswald and his father suggests what we later learn, that she is trying to see that Oswald inherits nothing from his father. As we afterward see, he has inherited too much. Oswald's reference to his father's good and useful life, and the Pastor's agreement, show how well Mrs. Alving guarded the secret of her husband's dissolute ways. The Pastor's moral indignation about Oswald and Mrs. Alving is rapidly deflated by the latter's revelation of her husband's continued debauchery.

The title of the play is applied at the very end of the act to suggest that Oswald and Regina appear almost like reincarnations of Captain Alving and Regina's mother. Ibsen will later expand his **theme** to include the traditional outmoded thoughts and values that rule Pastor Manders and contribute to the tragedy of Mrs. Alving.

GHOSTS

TEXTUAL ANALYSIS

ACT TWO

....

After dinner, Mrs. Alving and the Pastor talk over what to do with Regina, since as Oswald's half sister she cannot remain in the house. Mrs. Alving gives all of the details about the marriage of Regina's mother to Engstrand. The Pastor is shocked that the carpenter would marry a fallen woman for a few hundred dollars. Mrs. Alving counters that she married a fallen man. Manders fails to see any similarity in the two cases.

Mrs. Alving even considers allowing Regina to marry Oswald despite their relationship, but she cannot bring herself to do it. Manders applauds her for her scruples, but she maintains that only her cowardice keeps her from allowing Oswald and Regina to marry. She explains that all of us are ruled by "ghosts ... by dead ideas and dead beliefs." Manders still looks upon his stern rejection of Mrs. Alving when she tried to leave the Captain as the spiritual crisis of his life. To Mrs. Alving, now at least partly conscious of the extent to which the "ghosts" have ruled her, the matter seems a crime against them both, since she and Manders had loved one another before her ill-advised marriage to Alving.

Engstrand enters, only to be confronted by Manders, indignant that the carpenter never told the Pastor the truth about his marriage. The wily old scamp then proceeds to dupe Manders by telling how he did it only to raise up a poor fallen woman. After sufficient references to his own virtues, Engstrand enlists the Pastor's approval for the proposed seafarers' home. When Engstrand leaves, Mrs. Alving, moved by Manders' extreme simplicity, calls him a big baby and offers to kiss him. He is properly shocked.

Oswald enters dejectedly and tells his mother about his condition. From what he says Mrs. Alving realizes he has congenital syphilis, but Oswald is completely unaware that it was inherited. He feels that somewhere in his life among the artists, although he was extremely circumspect and apparently celibate, he contracted the disease.

Oswald, Regina, and Mrs. Alving drink champagne together. He is much impressed with Regina's physical attractiveness, and especially with her "joy of life." He explains what he means: that to people at home life is miserable, and work is drudgery to be endured, but in Paris life and work are things to be enjoyed. Mrs. Alving suddenly understands what Oswald means and how it applies to her: "Now I see how things happened." She is about to tell them the truth about themselves when Manders enters. He has just returned from the orphanage where he conducted an evening's prayer. When Oswald declares his intention of keeping Regina with him, Mrs. Alving forbids it and is about to give her reasons when word arrives that the orphanage is on fire. The blaze becomes visible from the window. They all rush outside to see it better.

Comment

Mrs. Alving's second use of the word "ghosts" is important, since it is the first statement of the real **theme** of the play. She is more ruled by these outmoded ideas and beliefs than she realizes. Her wish to build a Captain Alving Foundation stems from her desire to save appearances, to keep the rest of the world from knowing what her husband really was like. Her insistence that it be built with funds equal to her husband's entire estate is due to similar motives. She wants to keep Oswald from inheriting anything from his father.

Her wish is a good example of dramatic **irony**, which is an action or statement which carries one meaning to the actor and a different one to the audience. What she wants to do and what actually happens are completely opposite. She tries as hard as she can to keep anything of her husband from reappearing in Oswald. She denies any resemblance to the late Captain, and she insists upon Oswald's giving up his pipe for cigars, because the Captain preferred a pipe. But what she cannot keep from Oswald is the noncontagious aftereffect of her husband's venereal disease, which was transmitted to her son at birth. Thus Oswald's condition is not contagious but the paresis has already begun to take its toll. When Oswald tells his mother all about it, he mentions the headaches he had as a child and how they are gaining in intensity. He quotes the doctor who examined him as saying "The sins of the father are visited on the children," but as yet Oswald has no inkling of the truth about his father.

The most significant lines in this act are those in which Mrs. Alving shows her understanding of what Oswald means by the "joy of life." Mrs. Alving now realizes that at least some of the blame for her unfortunate marriage may be charged to her. The late Captain was full of the joy of life when he married, but Mrs. Alving was brought up to think only of duty and conventional modes of conduct. Without realizing it, she constantly acted as a damper upon her husband's spirited nature.

GHOSTS

TEXTUAL ANALYSIS

ACT THREE

....

Engstrand blames Manders for accidentally starting the fire at the orphanage, then offers to take the blame upon himself. Overcome by the carpenter's generosity, Manders agrees to help with the sailor's home. Elated, Engstrand tells Oswald and Mrs. Alving that he will call it "Chamberlain Alving's Home," and he promises that it will be worthy of the Chamberlain's memory.

Mrs. Alving then tells Oswald and Regina the truth about their father. Regina's reaction is typical of her frank, sensuous, and rather selfish nature. She will leave at once to make her own way. She will try to get some of the money from Engstrand and the Pastor, and, failing all else, she can always go to "Chamberlain Alving's Home." When warned of her probable ruin, she simply says "Oh! Pooh!" and leaves.

Oswald shows no sympathy for his late father, and not too much love for his mother. Now very ill, he tells her: "I have enough to do thinking about myself." Mrs. Alving tries to give him some hope. She promises that soon he will see the sun. He tells her of the dread he constantly feels over the way in which he must die, not quickly, but slowly. He will sink into a state of idiocy that may last for years until death finally puts an end to his condition. Rather than face such a degrading end, he has secured poison, which he asks her to give him as soon as his mind is gone. She objects, but he insists that she who gave him life should take it back again.

She agrees, and they both become calm again, while she speaks of how he will have a long rest at home with her. The rain stops and dawn breaks forth in bright sunlight. Oswald shrinks in his chair, without moving, eyes glazed, and dully repeats: "Mother, give me the sun." She frantically looks for the pills and as the curtain falls, stands staring at him terrified, unable to speak.

Comment

One of the finest examples of dramatic **irony** in the play is Engstrand's assurance that his sailor's home will be worthy of the late Mr. Alving's memory. There is no doubt that it will.

One objection to this play is the ease with which Engstrand deceives Manders. The carpenter seems almost like a traditional stage cheater rather than a well-portrayed character. Manders himself is excessively gullible, especially in this scene.

The "ghosts" **theme** is seen again at a more obvious level when Regina decides to fend for herself. In this respect she resembles her none-too-careful mother. Her end may possibly be not as fortunate.

The third and most emphatic statement of the extended "ghosts" theme comes when Oswald is unable to show anything more than pity for the memory of his father. When Mrs. Alving objects that a son ought to love his father no matter what happens, Oswald calls her position superstitious. Mrs. Alving then realizes how much she is still controlled by these "ghosts" despite her desperate attempts at liberation. When she asks him if he loves her, he simply answers that he knows her at least, but hardly knew his father.

The ending of the play is powerfully effective, although it has been condemned by some conservative critics as involving mercy-killing. Actually, Ibsen does not state what will happen, whether Mrs. Alving will administer the pills or not. Whenever Ibsen was asked this question, he grew extremely impatient and sometimes uncivil. The question is irrelevant, for once Oswald is dead, the tragedy of Mrs. Alving is complete. All that she lived and worked for, her son, is gone. She is left with nothing, not even the memory of his love, for before his mind was destroyed, he was still so sick as to be scarcely able to think of anyone but himself. Mrs. Alving's tragedy is that of a woman left completely alone, with only the "ghosts," the dead ideas and beliefs that still rise to strangle her. The physical "ghosts" of venereal disease is only a symbol of these same dead ideas and lifeless conventions. Pastor Manders lives for them, but his life is spiritually arid, entirely devoid of love in any sense of the word. Mrs. Alving lives for the love of her son. Despite her partial realization of their valuelessness, she still labors to follow her dead ideas and beliefs in maintaining her late husband's reputation and concealing the truth from her son and his half sister. Before the end of the drama, the whole edifice of falsehood she has erected, including its symbol, the orphanage, collapses.

GHOSTS

CHARACTERS ANALYSES

MRS. ALVING

Mrs. Alving is the central character of the play. It is her tragedy. She demonstrates tact and sensitiveness in her dealings with the Pastor, with whom she was in love before her marriage to Alving. Her poise and sweetness, as well as her vigorous courage, are displayed again and again. Our first impression is one of serenity; then we realize the somber depths of her character. Her great self-control enabled her to survive a marriage to a dissolute husband and build up their estate and his reputation into a lasting monument to his memory.

Her reading, as is suggested in the first and second acts, emancipated her intellectually from dead ideas and beliefs. Her feelings, however, do not keep pace with her intellectual freedom for, after all, she is still a woman with a woman's deep capacity for emotion. Therefore in practice she follows conventions; she guards the appearance of honor and respectability in her own way almost as much as Manders does in his. She is reluctant to tell her son the truth, even after his revelation of his disease. What finally makes her tell is his discussion of "joy of life."

Even then, she tries to gloss over her husband's faults, taking perhaps a little too much blame for herself. She and the dead beliefs that she was brought up with were certainly to blame, in that they repressed and frustrated Captain Alving's "joy of life." But that fact still does not excuse the Captain's utterly irresponsible behavior. On the other hand, Mrs. Alving's realization of her own deficiencies is important, since through it she gains much in tragic stature. In recognizing her own fault of character, she approaches that realization of self which is the basis of many great tragedies. For example, in Oedipus Rex, a Greek tragedy by Sophocles, the hero experiences a similar recognition of his own guilt.

OSWALD

Oswald, her son, at the beginning of the play already shows signs of intellectual and physical deterioration, although we are not told until the middle of the second act what disease he suffers from, and only near the very end of the play does Oswald indicate the precise extent of his illness. His unstable emotions are obvious, particularly in his sudden passion for Regina, and in his fluctuating gratitude toward his mother. Basically very simple and naive, Oswald views the world beyond Norway as bright and cheerful compared to the gloom of his native land. Although this judgment does to a certain extent reflect Ibsen's own feelings, in the context of the play it clearly evidences Oswald's unsophisticated nature.

PASTOR MANDERS

Pastor Manders is very much like the Dean in *Brand*, but with one exception. The Dean is obviously a politician in the worst sense of the word, more interested in self-advancement than in advancing the cause of the State Church. No one could accuse Manders of conscious hypocrisy, not even in the famous scene where he cautions Mrs. Alving about her reading habits. But he remains a hypocrite, even if only on the subconscious level. As the supposed guardian of morals for the community, he is eagerly concerned with keeping up the appearance of morality. Therefore he is easily duped by the rascally schemer Engstrand.

Manders thus is lacking in intellectual honesty. As for the ability of leadership which we would expect of a pastor, he has none. He is rather a follower of the herd. His sheep lead him. More worried about what the "really responsible people" think than about any higher moral principle, he rules his life and tries to rule others' lives according to what he thinks would be most acceptable socially. He has been successful enough at maintaining his prestige to develop a certain amount of smugness without any arrogance. Overall, however, his personality strikes us as rather bland. The contrast between his colorlessness and the tragic intensity of Mrs. Alving is extremely sharp.

JACOB ENGSTRAND

Jacob Engstrand, the carpenter, is very much a stock theatrical villain. He constantly boasts of his own virtue, although he has none, in such a way that only the gullible Manders is at all impressed. His hypocrisy is conscious and deliberate, calculated to make money, whereas Pastor Manders' hypocrisy or intellectual dishonesty is a quality of which he is not consciously aware. Engstrand's chief function in the play is to serve as a foil or contrasting character to the Pastor.

AN ENEMY OF THE PEOPLE

INTRODUCTION

Ibsen was motivated to write this play by the universal condemnation of his previous effort *Ghosts* by both conservative and liberal forces. Ibsen maintained an outward calm, and gradually his anger and resentment at the critics changed into a rather caustic humor. To defend his own position he wrote *An Enemy of the People* within one year instead of the usual two. The play deals with a rather bumbling but well-intentioned reformer, Dr. Stockmann, who becomes a mouthpiece for some of Ibsen's own ideas.

Unlike *Ghosts*, with its tragic **theme**, *An Enemy of the People* is a fast - moving comedy. Ibsen probably so conceived it to make it a better vehicle for his **theme**, since things move so rapidly that the audience has no opportunity to question either the logic of the plot or the truth of the ideas expressed. The basic **theme** of the play is similar to that of *Ghosts*. Dr. Stockmann discovers first that the baths upon which the resort town depends are polluted. Then he realizes that the minds of the people are polluted as well, by outmoded ideas and dead beliefs. Therefore we can observe Ibsen presenting the same **theme** in a near tragedy, *Ghosts*, as well as in a successful comedy, *An Enemy of the People*.

From its first performance in 1882 until the present, this play has been one of Ibsen's most effective pieces in the theatre, and one of his most widely read. It is well worth mentioning that when the eminent American playwright Arthur Miller, a great admirer of Ibsen, decided to adapt one of the Norwegian playwright's works he chose *An Enemy of the People*.

CHARACTERS

Doctor Thomas Stockmann, Medical Officer for the Municipal Baths.

Mrs. Katherine Stockmann, his wife.

Petra, their daughter, a schoolteacher.

Ejlif, their elder son, aged thirteen.

Morten, their younger son, aged ten.

Peter Stockmann, the Doctor's elder brother; Mayor and Chief Constable of the town; Chairman of the Committee for the Baths.

Morten Kiil, owner of a tannery and Mrs. Stockmann's adoptive father.

Hovstad, editor of the "People's Messenger," a self-styled liberal newspaper.

Billing, his subeditor.

Captain Horster, a friend of the Stockmanns.

Aslaksen, owner of a small print shop.

Miscellaneous Men, Women, And Schoolboys.

The setting is a small coastal town in southern Norway. Acts One and Two take place in Doctor Stockmann's sitting room; Act Three in the office of the "People's Messenger"; Act Four in a big room in Captain Horster's house; Act Five in Doctor Stockmann's study.

AN ENEMY OF THE PEOPLE

TEXTUAL ANALYSIS

ACT ONE

....

The Stockmanns have just finished an evening meal, and a few late guests arrive, first Billing, junior editor of the "People's Messenger," a local paper, then Peter Stockmann, the Mayor of the town and Doctor Stockmann's elder brother. Billing immediately starts eating, but the Mayor declines, commenting on the excessiveness of having hot beef at night. The next arrival is the editor Hovstad. The Mayor has a few words of praise for Hovstad's paper, and a great deal of praise for the new Baths, for the organization of which he assumes the principal share of credit, despite Doctor Stockmann's efforts in proposing and designing the Baths.

The Doctor enters with his two young sons and Captain Horster, a friend. All sit down for some hot toddy except the boys, who are too young, and the Mayor, whose digestion admits of neither beef nor liquor. The Doctor boasts a little to his brother about how well they are getting along; for he is making almost as much as they are spending. Doctor Stockmann suggests to his brother that there may be some difficulty concerning the Baths, but the Mayor replies that any reports or arrangements must be made through the proper channels.

After the Mayor leaves, the Doctor, Captain Horster, Hovstad, and Billing converse. The first topic is politics, about which the Captain is ignorant and indifferent. The two editors are shocked and utter a few patriotic sentiments. The topic of discussion next shifts to the Baths. Petra, the daughter, returns from her day's work at the school, bringing a letter for her father. While the Doctor retires to his study to read the letter, Petra and the editors demonstrate their liberal opinions about politics and religion.

Doctor Stockmann returns, announcing a great discovery. The Baths are polluted by waste matter from the nearby tanneries which flows into the reservoir as well as down into the ocean near the bathing beach. Thus both drinking and bathing water are contaminated. The Doctor has their maid bring a letter to his brother the Mayor, in which he explains the matter and insists that the intake pipe for the Baths will have to be relaid beyond the tanneries. The Doctor is elated by his discovery, and Hovstad and Billing feel that the town should give him some sort of testimonial. The act ends with the Doctor gleefully dancing about with his wife Katherine in his arms.

Comment

Ibsen presents his **exposition** in an interesting and entertaining manner, by means of an after-dinner social gathering. The tone of this first act is regulated by Doctor Stockmann's own optimistic and happy personality. He sparkles with joy and good feelings. His high spirits are contagious, so that the only person not affected is his elder brother Peter, the Mayor, whose solidly conservative bureaucratic outlook on life serves as a sharp contrast to the Doctor's effervescence. We also see evidence of Peter's shrewdness, in his careful praise for the two editors. He knows very well how to influence people.

The two editors deserve a little explanation. In their conversation with Captain Horster, they are patriotic, and in speaking to Petra, they are modern, liberal thinkers. Ibsen gives no hint at present as to how sincere they are, but their true characters are very soon made known.

Although this first act is good moderately-paced comedy, Ibsen includes first of all a little **foreshadowing** (suggestion of future events), when the Mayor suggests that some day his brother Thomas, the Doctor, may learn to his cost how important it is for the individual to obey his lawful superiors. Secondly, Ibsen includes a little dramatic **irony**, in which the speaker's words contain a meaning unsuspected by himself. An example of this is Billing's suggestion that the town give the Doctor some sort of testimonial. The testimonial that the Doctor finally gets is not what anyone has in mind at this time. Also rather ironic is the Doctor's insistence that he will refuse any salary increase even if the Baths Committee insists on it.

AN ENEMY OF THE PEOPLE

TEXTUAL ANALYSIS

ACT TWO

Act Two (the next morning). Mrs. Stockmann's adoptive father Morten Kiil comes in, chuckling with merriment over the Doctor's theory of the "little animals" that no one can see infesting the water supply. Since he has a grudge against the town fathers, he hopes that the Doctor will stick to his story so as to embarrass the whole Baths Committee. He is afraid, however, that the Mayor may not be foolish enough to believe the story.

Hovstad next arrives, spouting moral sentiments on truth and freedom, and complaining that the true poison is not the Baths but the self-centered group of officials and elder citizens who run the town. He denies any personal motives, but he does suggest that the humble and oppressed people should be emancipated, and that he as a journalist will undertake the task. His conscience, he insists, is clear.

The printer Aslaksen then comes. He preaches his usual doctrine of moderation, cautioning both Hovstad and the Doctor against discourtesy to the authorities. The compact majority of small tradesmen will, he promises, be on the side of the Doctor. Hovstad is not impressed, and he insists that a man should be self-reliant and sure of himself instead of weak like the printer. The editor is determined to print an article about the Baths, but the Doctor extracts a promise from him not to do so unless the Mayor refuses to correct the situation. Doctor Stockmann is elated to see that the press and the tradesmen are on his side. When he tells his wife that the compact majority is with him, she asks him if that really is a good thing.

The Mayor enters. He is upset about the report on the Baths, first because it was delivered after office hours, second because it was done behind his back, and third because the proposed improvements would be enormously expensive and take two years to complete. Peter Stockmann is sure that his brother's report is exaggerated. When the Doctor places the blame squarely upon the Mayor's insistence on locating the Baths and the intake pipes where they now are, Peter's defense is very simple. He informs his brother Thomas that it is in the public interest to defend the reputation of officials like himself. Therefore he insists that Thomas Stockmann's report be kept secret, to be acted upon by the Mayor and other officials as they see fit. Finally, he threatens the Doctor with dismissal if he does not make a public retraction of his views on the Baths. As he leaves, he states that anyone who could have such offensive ideas about the town must be an enemy of the community. The Doctor remains unshaken. He will not give in to the Mayor's demands regardless of consequences.

Comment

The prediction of old Morten Kiil, nicknamed "the Badger," that the Mayor will not believe the story about the Baths, comes true. On the other hand, his motives in hoping that it would have been believed were strictly personal. Equally self-interested is the editor Hovstad, who protests altogether too much about his disinterested motives and his clear conscience. Aslaksen's assurance about the "compact majority" seems to comfort the Doctor, but Katherine Stockmann's seemingly naive question about its worth is really one of the most brilliant lines in the play. It does not take long for us to see just how good the compact majority is for Doctor Stockmann.

Peter Stockman's motives are quite obvious. First and foremost he is concerned with keeping his position, and for it he will sacrifice anyone, even his own brother's welfare and the lives of countless visitors to the Baths. One of his comments is particularly appropriate. When he criticizes his brother's writing about one new idea after another, he states that the people do not need any new ideas; the old established ones are better for them.

AN ENEMY OF THE PEOPLE

TEXTUAL ANALYSIS

ACT THREE

In their newspaper office Hovstad and Billing discuss how no matter what happens they should profit by the situation, until with their paper as a weapon they can discredit the Mayor and eventually secure the town offices for themselves.

Doctor Stockmann brings in his report on the Baths to be published word for word. He is determined to fight his brother and any other incapable officials, in order to purify not only the Baths, but also the entire social life of the town. Hovstad and Billing encourage him while Aslaksen preaches moderation.

After the Doctor leaves, Aslaksen gives the two editors a brief talk about politics, in which he declares himself a liberal in national affairs, where no one is harmed by it, but very moderate in local affairs, where opposition to officials only hurts oneself. He reminds them that the previous editor of the paper proved himself a turncoat, and he remarks on Billing's having applied for a local government position.

Petra brings in an English story which the editors wanted her to translate for them. She refuses because it is a fiction in which the good are rewarded and the bad are punished. Hovstad explains that since their readers like such stories they print them. Petra is disappointed by his lack of principles, and then disgusted when he makes an obvious play for her affections by suggesting that he supported Doctor Stockmann only because of her. Thoroughly disillusioned with him, she takes her leave.

The next arrival on the scene is the Mayor, who informs Aslaksen and Hovstad that any improvements in the Baths will have to be made by the small tradesmen, since the owners of the Baths cannot afford any further expense. Horrified by the thought of higher taxes, both agree with Peter Stockmann that the Doctor's report must be untrue. The two of them agree to print the Mayor's statement instead of the Doctor's.

As the Mayor hurriedly leaves the room, Thomas Stockmann returns, eager to see the proofs of his article. He insists that no demonstration be made in his honor. Katherine then comes in looking for him, and she blames the editors for trying to dupe him. But the Doctor remains optimistic and happy. When he sees his brother's official hat and staff, he picks them up and parades about the office, to everyone's embarrassment by his own. The Mayor enters in a rage, and all turn against the Doctor except his own wife. The printer and the editors all accuse the Doctor of misrepresentation or worse. Undaunted, Thomas Stockmann intends to read his paper in public, and goes off to make preparations.

Comment

In this act, Ibsen gives his first statement of the **theme** when Doctor Stockmann declares that the entire social life of the town needs to be cleansed, not just the Baths. Ibsen uses dramatic **irony** again when Aslaksen and the editors at first declare him a friend of the community, and then turn against him once the Mayor applies a little economic pressure.

Peter Stockmann's lack of scruples is clear when he tells Aslaksen and Hovstad that any extensive repairs to the Baths must be paid out of municipal funds, since the legality of such a course is at best questionable. Both fall for the trick and are immediately on the side of the Mayor. Although we are not told what the Mayor said to Billing, it was equally effective.

AN ENEMY OF THE PEOPLE

TEXTUAL ANALYSIS

ACT FOUR

The townspeople assemble in a room in Captain Horster's house, the only place Doctor Stockmann could find to deliver his public lecture. The entire Stockmann family is present, as well as the Mayor, Aslaksen, Hovstad, Billing, and most of the compact majority of tradesmen and landowners. Before the Doctor can start, Aslaksen is elected chairman by acclaim. After the printer's usual speech on moderation, Peter Stockmann moves that the Doctor be denied permission to speak about the Baths. Aslaksen and Hovstad both support the motion, but the Doctor assets that his topic has nothing to do with the poisoned Baths.

Doctor Stockmann then begins his lecture, with frequent interruptions from the crowd. He states his major contention that the entire social framework of the community is founded upon falsehood. He places the blame for this situation not upon slow-witted and prejudiced officials like his brother, but squarely upon the compact majority itself. When Hovstad and Billing insist that the majority always has truth and right on its side, the Doctor replies that the majority will accept only outmoded, time-worn ideas as true. The Doctor insists that the minority is always in the right, and that the majority is responsible for poisoning the moral life of the community.

To support his contention, Thomas Stockmann presents the example of animals. the well-bred fowl is more productive and the well-bred poodle more intelligent than any common examples of their species. He then suggests that the same principle is applicable to humans. The true people, then, is not the compact majority but rather the intellectual minority.

When accused of wanting to ruin the community, Doctor Stockmann answers that he would sooner destroy the town than see it prospering upon a foundation of filth and lies (that is, the polluted Baths). Infuriated members of the audience call him "an enemy of the people." After due preparations, the chairman Aslaksen calls for a vote on the matter, and a resolution is passed declaring the Doctor "an enemy of the people." With a few cheers for Aslaksen and the Mayor, and a number of insults for the Doctor, the meeting is adjourned.

Comment

In this act, Ibsen satirizes the workings of a democracy in which the compact majority seems to have the final word. The Doctor presents the major **theme** of the play, that society is poisoned by the majority's blind acceptance of outmoded beliefs and worn-out ideas. The Doctor's trust in an intellectual minority parallels Ibsen's own thoughts on the subject. Like the nineteenth-century English philosopher John Stuart Mill (1806-1873), Ibsen believed in a sort of aristocracy of the intellect.

Ibsen's distrust of the compact liberal majority mirrors his discontent with the contemporary political situation in Norway, particularly with the popular liberal party led by the Norwegian politician Johan Sverdrup, who Ibsen felt was a do-nothing. The best short discussion of the complex political background of this play is by Brian W. Downs in his *Ibsen*, pp. 170 - 5 (see Bibliography).

AN ENEMY OF THE PEOPLE

TEXTUAL ANALYSIS

ACT FIVE

Act Five (the next day). Doctor Stockmann is in his study, which is disordered. All the windows are broken. As he picks a stone up off the floor, Mrs. Stockmann brings a notice from the landlord, who does not dare do otherwise than ask them to leave. The Doctor decides to go with Captain Horster to America. He wants to leave the place where his windows were broken and his best trousers torn. As he puts it, one should never wear his best trousers when he goes out fighting for truth and justice.

Petra comes home early, having been dismissed because her superior did not dare do otherwise. Captain Horster loses his position as ship's captain, because the owner felt he dared not do otherwise. Finally, Peter Stockmann, brings in a letter of dismissal for his brother, because he dares not do otherwise. He holds out hope for his brother's possible reinstatement, provided the latter retracts his position on the Baths.

The Mayor warns his brother of the precarious financial position in which the latter now finds himself. Morten Kiil's fortune, the Mayor tells him, is to go to Mrs. Stockmann and the boys, but the old tanner could always change his will. The Doctor replies that "the Badger is too pleased with his attacks on the Mayor and his associates ever to change his mind. Peter Stockmann now sees what he considers to be his brother's real motives. He feels that Thomas agreed to attack the Baths in order to assure getting Morten Kiil's money. He leaves, confident now that he has a weapon to use against his brother.

The next visitor is Morten Kiil, who has been buying up all the shares of stock in the Baths he could get with the money that was supposed to go to Mrs. Stockmann and the boys. He gives the Doctor until two in the afternoon to retract his statements about the Baths, or to do anything else that will reclaim them.

The next guests are Hovstad and Aslaksen, who apologize for turning against the Doctor the day before. They say they could not do otherwise. They suggest that someone other than his father-in-law should have bought up the shares, perhaps they themselves. They offer to put the paper at the Doctor's disposal, as well as the services of Aslaksen's Householders' Association and Temperance Society, provided they get a share of the profits. In a brilliantly comic scene, the aroused Doctor Stockmann grabs his umbrella and beats them both out of the house.

Doctor Stockmann now is determined to fight for truth and freedom at home; he will not give in to the compact majority. At this moment the two boys come home early, dismissed from school because the schoolmaster feels that they should stay home for a day or two. This gives the Doctor an idea. He decides to open a school to teach his own sons and whatever poor boys in the town need an education. He now realizes that he is the strongest man in the town, because "the strongest man in the world is the one who stands most alone." With this new discovery of the Doctor's the play ends.

Comment

As this act begins, Doctor Stockmann is just cleaning up the last few rocks thrown in by common people outside. Having thus survived the assault by the rabble he, or rather his integrity of character, is then subjected to three successive assaults. Interspersed with these major assaults are the relatively minor matters of the eviction notice, Petra's dismissal, and the boys' return from school. The schoolmaster's name is Rorlund, just as in *Pillars of Society*, an earlier play by Ibsen.

The first of the three assaults is made by the Major who shows his own moral turpitude by seizing upon the erroneous conclusion that his brother Thomas is in league with Morten Kiil. Doctor Stockmann's father-in-law is the next tempter. He presents the alternatives: either restore the reputation and value of the Baths or lose all of the fortune destined for Mrs. Stockmann and the two boys. The Doctor again refuses any compromise short of the truth.

The last and most subtle tempters are the two opportunists Hovstad and Aslaksen. Their failure is much more spectacular and amusing. The Doctor maintains his integrity, and audience sympathy as well, so that his final line usually receives an appropriate degree of applause.

Through this fast-paced high comedy, Ibsen presents his basic **theme** that society is poisoned by the outmoded ideas and beliefs nourished by the compact majority. Several problems are left unsolved or unanswered. Because of the pace of the comedy, the audience tends to give its sympathy wholly to the Doctor in his fight for truth and freedom. We do not consider, for example, the impact of the Doctor's insistence on truth upon the community as a whole. That the ruin of the Baths means ruin for the economic life of the town never crosses our minds. In his next play, *The Wild Duck*, Ibsen investigates the evil effects of such an uncompromising quest for ideal truth, as he did earlier in *Brand*.

AN ENEMY OF THE PEOPLE

CHARACTERS ANALYSES

DOCTOR THOMAS STOCKMANN

Doctor Thomas Stockmann is a reformer and a constant fighter for the ideals of truth and freedom. A true liberal, he opposes any attempt to curtail his freedom of expression. As his brother puts it, he is independent and impetuous. The Doctor is the sort of man who nearly always runs afoul of authorities by speaking his own mind regardless of consequences. Ibsen has made his character very appealing, however, by giving him a number of human faults. Thomas Stockmann is optimistic and happy to the point of being easily duped by others. An example of this is the way in which he is used by Hovstad and Billing for their political schemes. His optimism forces him always to look on the bright side of things, and his concern for ideals causes him to lose sight of details. When in the last act his wife reminds him of their lack of income now that he is dismissed, he simply tells her that she will have to save a little more here and there and they will get along. It is this unconquerably cheerful optimism that makes this play a successful comedy.

PETER STOCKMANN

Peter Stockmann, the Doctor's elder brother, is very much like Ibsen's other petty officials, for example, the Mayor in *Brand*. Representing the conservative, vested interests in the town, he has no tolerance for his brother's liberal point of view, and uses any means in his power to try to force the Doctor to come to terms. Peter is stodgy and unimaginative, yet at the same time he is shrewd in dealing with others.

HOVSTAD

Hovstad, the editor of the "People's Messenger," is an opportunist and timeserver. At the beginning of the play he and his associate Billing display liberal ideas and beliefs, yet once the Mayor applies a little economic pressure, Hovstad turns against his former friend and accuses him of misrepresentation. Although he is a freethinker at the Stockmann's house, he is thoroughly conventional in his editing of the paper. He supports the Doctor only as long as it seems that the Doctor might win the struggle with the Mayor.

ASLAKSEN

Aslaksen is representative of Ibsen's **satire** against middle-class mediocrity and shallowness. The printer never fails to preach moderation. Even when the Doctor beats him out of the house, he howls the same word.

THE WILD DUCK

INTRODUCTION

Ibsen wrote this play in 1884 as an answer to *An Enemy of the People*, just as that play answered the critics of *Ghosts*. But in *The Wild Duck*, Ibsen seems to focus upon himself; at least that was the interpretation given to the play by its contemporary critics, as well as by many recent scholars. In Doctor Thomas Stockmann, Ibsen presents a well-intentioned idealist and reformer who is rather bumbling and easily taken advantage of. The message of that play centers on the necessity for truth and freedom, for which the Doctor would make any sacrifice needed, of himself, his family, and his town. In *The Wild Duck* Ibsen concerns himself with the life-lie or life-illusion which seems necessary to bolster up some people's lives. The idealist in this play is Gregers Werle, whose stupid attempts to satisfy his craving for truth lead eventually to tragedy.

The major difficulties in interpreting this play are two. To begin with, the plot seems at first glance to have no central character. A closer reading, however, suggests what Ibsen is trying to do. He attempts in this play to give an objective picture of a group of interrelated characters in a domestic scene. His attitude towards all the persons of his drama except Gregers Werle is detached. Only for the idealist Gregers does Ibsen reserve his scorn. Even the tragic conclusion of the play is handled with a degree of detachment that maintains the dominant comic rather than tragic tone. Although the play is basically a comedy with serious overtones and a tragic conclusion, it is sardonic and often bitter, especially in the treatment of Gregers Werle.

The second and more serious problem concerns the symbolism in the play. Ibsen himself remarked that he gave the critics a few things to fight about and interpret. Most of the squabbling has been over the meaning of the central image, the wild duck. The following are the most common interpretations:

1. It represents Gregers Werle, the idealist who fails.

2. It represents any such idealist whose aspirations are misplaced.

3. It represents Hialmar Ekdal, limited by marriage and parenthood, and saddled with a business (photography) in which he has no real interest. This interpretation is suggested by Gregers in the text.

4. It represents Ekdal Senior, broken in mind and weakened in body, whose only contact with the bright world of nature is in the model woods set up in Ekdal's attic.

5. It represents Ibsen's own reforming and moralizing spirit.

6. It represents the social castaways in the play: the outcast Gregers, the pretentious Hialmar, the tipsy play-hunter old Ekdal, the washed-out Doctor Relling, and the alcoholic theology student Molvik.

Good arguments can be presented for any of the above interpretations, yet no one really presents the final word on the subject. The reason for this interpretative problem is that Ibsen developed a habit in his later plays of manipulating his symbols so as to give them plural values. The result is often confusing to the reader, and critics have sometimes considered this habit one of the major structural faults of Ibsen's later dramas.

CHARACTERS

Werle, a wealthy merchant and manufacturer.

Gregers Werle (pronounced Gray-gers Ver-luh), his son.

Old Ekdal, a retired army officer.

Hialmar Ekdal (pronounced Yalmar), his son, a photographer.

Gina Ekdal (pronounced with hard "g").

Hedwig, their daughter, fourteen years old.

Mrs. Sorby, Werle's housekeeper.

Doctor Relling

Molvik, a student of theology.

Graberg (pronounced Groberg), Werle's bookkeeper.

Pettersen, Werle's servant; Jensen, a hired waiter; Gentlemen; Hired Waiters.

The setting in Act One is Werle's house. Acts Two through Five are in Hialmar Ekdal's home.

THE WILD DUCK

TEXTUAL ANALYSIS

ACT ONE

．．

The play opens with the servants straightening up Werle's study. They discuss how the dinner now being served in the next room is for Gregers, old Werle's son who has been away from home for years at a distant factory. They mention how old Werle and the housekeeper are good friends.

Old Ekdal hurries through on his way to the office. Then the guests come in from the dining room, on their way to the music room for dessert. Werle pointedly remarks that there were thirteen of them at the table. Hialmar Ekdal, Gregers' old friend from college, was the outsider. Gregers and Hialmar then talk about what has happened in the seventeen years since they last met. Hialmar mentions his father's disgrace and ruin, and his prison sentence. Werle then set up Hialmar in business as a photographer. Gregers' father also made it possible for Hialmar to marry Gina Hansen, a former maid at the Werle house.

Mrs. Sorby enters with Werle, cautioning him not to look at the bright lights. The other guests come in, and Hialmar is brought into a conversation about Tokay wine, of which he knows nothing.

Graberg the bookkeeper and Old Ekdal then pass through on their way home, since the keys to the office are missing and the only other way out leads through the study. The appearance of the eccentric old Ekdal with his dirty red wig startles all of the guests. Hialmar turns aside, pretending not to know his father. The idealistic Gregers is shocked. Hialmar then takes his leave. Gregers promises to visit him soon, but young Ekdal would prefer to meet his old friend somewhere in town.

The rest of the act is devoted to a heated discussion between the Werles. They speak about the Ekdals, and Werle Senior practically admits that he was equally guilty with Old Ekdal of the offense that ruined the latter and sent him to jail. But Werle insists he was acquitted. We learn that Werle Senior has since practically supported the Ekdals by his liberal payment to Old Ekdal for occasional copying work. Gregers seems particularly incensed over the matter of Gina, his father's former mistress now married to Hialmar. To Gregers, this is the last of a series of insults to his mother, to whom he was inordinately attached, and from whom he learned to hate his father. Accordingly he has no sympathy for his father's weakened eyesight, and no desire either to assist or to oppose Werle's plans to marry Mrs. Sorby. As he leaves, Gregers says that he now knows his mission in life, but he does not explain.

Comment

As usual, Ibsen gradually unfolds his **exposition** or disclosure of basic facts. We are introduced to the Werles and to Hialmar. At this point, the latter seems a shy and unobtrusive young man, obviously out of place since he was the thirteenth at the table.

Mrs. Sorby's warning to Werle about the bright lights, and the latter's admission to his son about his failing eyesight anticipate the connection later to be divulged between the elder Werle and Hedwig, the Ekdals' daughter.

The discussion between the Werles is important for two reasons. It supplies the reader with needed information about Werle Senior's relations with the Ekdals and Mrs. Sorby. Even more important is the light that is shed on young Werle's character. His hatred for his father and near idolatry for the memory of his mother suggest his unbalanced psychological state. Thus Ibsen supplies him with the basic ingredients of an Oedipus complex.

THE WILD DUCK

TEXTUAL ANALYSIS

ACT TWO

Gina and Hedwig are sitting in the Ekdals' studio. Gina warns her daughter not to read too long. They talk over the day's expenses and receipts. Old Ekdal comes in with a packet of copying work and another package, obviously a bottle, and retires to his room.

Hialmar comes in and tells them about the excellent banquet and how he gave them all a good lecture on wines, and outwitted the wealthy guests in the conversations. Hedwig is disappointed for a moment when Hialmar fails to bring her a dainty from the feast. When he learns about how slow business is, he enthusiastically announces his intention of working very hard tomorrow, but a bottle of beer soon cures him of his fervor. He begins to play the flute, but is interrupted by a knocking at the door.

Gregers enters. The discussion turns to Hedwig's approaching blindness, which Gina Ekdal says is inherited from Hialmar's mother. This topic makes Hialmar sad, but he is soon cheered by beer and bread and butter. The Ekdals show Gregers their attic in which they keep pigeons, rabbits, chickens, and a wounded wild duck. Old Ekdal explains how Werle Senior shot at the duck, which then plunged into the water all the way to the bottom, entangling itself in weeds. Werle's dog retrieved the duck, which was eventually given to Hialmar's father.

Gregers arranges to rent a spare room from the Ekdals despite Gina's unwillingness. With the remark that he would prefer to be a clever dog that dives after and rescues wild ducks, he leaves. His remark mystifies Gina and Hedwig. The latter states that Gregers seemed to mean something other than what he said all the time. Hialmar sits down to his bread and butter. He tells Gina and Hedwig not to worry about anything, just to rely on him, for he means to fulfill his mission in life. Gina agrees, but suggests that meanwhile they carry Old Ekdal, who has fallen asleep, off to bed.

Comment

The frequent **allusions** in this act to Hedwig's weak eyes reinforce the suggestion that she may be old Werle's daughter. Gina, however, insists that the blindness is inherited from Hialmar's mother. Ibsen never openly states whether Hedwig is or is not Werle's daughter. This is another of those things the author said the critics would squabble over.

Hialmar's flute-playing as much as his subsequent melancholy over Hedwig's sight is evidence of how much he enjoys being the center of little family scenes of domestic happiness. When the topic turns to Hedwig he, perhaps subconsciously, becomes melancholy until the offer of beer turns the focus back upon him. Thus our shy and retiring Hialmar of the first act is seen to be very much of a poseur (one who affects a particular pose to impress others). This impression is verified by the elaborate lies he tells about his conversation at the dinner.

Old Ekdal's description of the shooting of the wild duck is important, because it forms the basis of most of the symbols later used by Gregers in speaking of his quest. Gregers immediately begins to speak in mysteries. His message goes completely over the head of Hialmar, but Hedwig at least realizes that there is some hidden meaning behind much of what Gregers says. The final scene is an excellent comment on Hialmar's constant boasting of what he will do in the future. Gina simply makes him return to the comparatively drab present.

THE WILD DUCK

TEXTUAL ANALYSIS

ACT THREE

Act Three (the next morning). Gregers has just gone out after making a mess of his room trying to light a fire in his stove. Hialmar has invited him and the other roomers, Relling and Molvik, to lunch. Gina asks Hialmar to retouch some photographs while she prepares lunch. He starts to work rather lazily, then joins his father in the attic, where they busy themselves repairing the animals' quarters.

Gregers comes in and holds a long conversation with Hedwig about the attic and its principal inhabitant, the wild duck. She describes the old furniture and books in the attic, which she has become accustomed to calling "the depths of the sea." When Gregers uses the same phrase, each finds a responsive chord in the other. When Hedwig laughs and says it is only an attic, he asks her if she is really certain.

As Gina comes in, they hear firing from within the attic. Hialmar comes out carrying a pistol. He puts it on a bookcase and warns Hedwig about it, since one barrel is still loaded. He then describes his invention to Gregers, although he has not progressed sufficiently to give him any details. He does expand optimistically on the great future the invention will assure him. Every afternoon after dinner he shuts himself in the parlor and meditates on his invention. Gregers then says that like the wild duck, Hialmar has dived into a poisonous marsh. Young Ekdal is upset because no one ever talks about unpleasant things in his house.

Relling and Molvik then come in. Doctor Relling remembers Gregers when they both were at the same factory. He tells how Gregers went about to the homes of the people presenting a "claim of the ideal." Gregers states that he still carries it in his breast. The Doctor warns him not to try to present it here or he will kick him down the stairs.

Werle then comes in to warn his son not to make any trouble for the Ekdals. Gregers, however, is determined to tell Hialmar the whole truth about his marriage. He reproaches his father for ruining Old Ekdal. Werle, in turn, tells Gregers that the latter will never find any relief for his sick conscience, since it is a legacy from his mother. Werle Senior then leaves after announcing his intention of marrying Mrs. Sorby and offering Gregers a share of his fortune. Gregers refuses and will have nothing further to do with his father. Hialmar goes out for a walk with Gregers, despite the warnings from both Gina and Doctor Relling. The latter states that Gregers suffers from a disease known as "acute integrity."

Comment

Gregers' complete inability to make a fire and the mess he makes of his room suggest the futility and destructiveness of what Doctor Relling later refers to as his "claim of the ideal." Hialmar's utter indifference to productive work is completely in character. Although he refers to himself as a hardworking breadwinner, it is obvious that Gina and even Hedwig with her poor eyesight do more work than he does.

The sympathy that Hedwig and Gregers seem to feel for each other prepares the way for the young girl's assuming the role that the idealist suggests to her in the last act, her last supreme self-sacrifice. The warning that Hialmar gives her about the pistol is a technical preparation for Hedwig's suicide. The fact of the gun's being ready and loaded is established, as well as her knowledge of its location.

Hialmar refers to his after-dinner periods of meditation on his invention, but Gina always simply calls this period his nap time. Hialmar's reaction to Gregers' promptings and suggestions is one of uneasiness, for he prefers to hear only pleasant things. His curiosity finally gets the better of him when he goes out for the walk, although his motive seems to be more to help Gregers than to learn anything.

Young Werle's determination to place Hialmar's marriage on a basis of truth reminds us of *A Doll's House, Ghosts*, and *Pillars of Society*, all dealing with marriages not based on truth. Hialmar, however seems quite content with what he has; his only concern is to avoid unpleasantness.

The final comment of Doctor Relling requires some explanation. The original reads "en akut retskaffenhedsfeber." The usual translation of "acute integrity" or "probity" or "uprightness" is hardly adequate. The most brilliant translation of this phrase is by the critic and scholar Otto Heller (see Bibliography), who calls it "acute rectitudinitis."

THE WILD DUCK

TEXTUAL ANALYSIS

ACT FOUR

While Hialmar is out, Gina and Hedwig carry on the photographic business as they always do. He returns and refuses to eat any dinner. He announces that starting the day after next, since tomorrow is Hedwig's birthday, he will take all of the business as well as all of the household accounts into his own hands. He cries out that he would like to wring the wild duck's neck, but he spares it for Hedwig's sake. He sends Hedwig out for a walk, and then confronts Gina with the facts he has just learned about their marriage, although he so far does not doubt that Hedwig is his child. He repeats such phrases as "claim of the ideal," and "swamp of deceit" that he learned from Gregers.

Gregers enters, surprised to see that Hialmar has not yet magnificently forgiven his wife. At this point Doctor Relling comes in. He cautions them all about Hedwig, saying that the child might even do an injury to herself or perhaps others if she is brought into the situation.

Mrs. Sorby brings in a letter from Werle to Hedwig. She explains to them how she is about to marry Werle and take care of him now that he is going blind. Hialmar notices this reference to blindness. When Gregers threatens to tell his father about Mrs. Sorby's former friendship with Doctor Relling, she answers that each of them has told the other everything. Hialmar grandiosely insists that she tell Werle Senior that all of the money given to the Ekdals will be paid back with interest from the proceeds of his invention.

When Hedwig returns, Hialmar opens the letter for her and reads it. It is a notice of a legacy to provide an income for Old Ekdal and for Hedwig after his death. Encouraged by Gregers, Hialmar makes the noble gesture of tearing the letter in half and placing the pieces on the table. The letter in addition to Hedwig's blindness convinces him of her true parentage. Weeping because no longer has he either home or child, he calls for his hat, cries for Hedwig to stay away from him, and takes his leave.

While Gina is out looking for Hialmar, Gregers suggests to Hedwig that she herself sacrifice the wild duck for her father as a "free-will offering." She agrees to do so the next morning.

Comment

Although Hialmar is perfectly sincere in his confrontation of his wife, he is extremely melodramatic. What he cannot understand is her comparatively unemotional reaction to the situation. As she puts it, she was too busy making a home for him and running the business to worry about the basis of their marriage. Hialmar's love of theatrical poses is most evident in his very dramatic tearing of the letter. What he needs to do is to dramatize himself, to create a scene in which he is, as always, the center, to enjoy it, then to relapse into ordinary routines again.

The Doctor's warning about Hedwig appears a little forced. It is hardly called for, but it does prepare for her suicide. Ibsen is always careful to lay all of the necessary groundwork for his conclusions.

Gregers' surprise at Hialmar's ungenerous conduct is to be expected, since he still admires Hialmar, considering him a "wild duck" capable of soaring high, in a spiritual sense. But young Ekdal, as we have already seen, is too much attached to his beer and bread and butter to fly in any sense of the word.

At the end of the act, Gregers literally intends that Hedwig should sacrifice her wild duck. But as early as the end of the second act, Hedwig is aware that he often means more than he says. It is possible, then, that further reflection upon his words may induce thoughts of suicide.

THE WILD DUCK

TEXTUAL ANALYSIS

ACT FIVE

Act Five (the next morning). Relling comes in to tell the Ekdals and Gregers that Hialmar spent the night with him and is presently snoring on a couch downstairs. The Doctor tells Gregers what Hialmar's problem is. Having been raised by two maiden aunts, young Ekdal was always the center of admiration. Superficial and sentimental, he has a great talent for declamation. Relling continues by analyzing Gregers, who in his search for the ideal admits that he must try to find it outside himself. The Doctor tells Gregers that the only way for life to be bearable for people like Hialmar and the alcoholic Molvik is for them to cultivate a "life-lie," an illusion by which one maintains a degree of self-respect. As Relling insists, if a man's life-lie is taken from him, so is his happiness.

After Relling leaves, Gregers again encourages Hedwig to sacrifice the wild duck. She asks her grandfather how to shoot a wild duck, and he tells her how. She fingers the pistol on the bookcase, but puts it down hurriedly when Gina enters.

Hialmar returns, unwashed and unkempt. He repulses Hedwig and calls at once for his scientific magazines so that he can work on his invention. Determined to leave, he refuses to eat salt meat even though he is careful to declare that he has not eaten for nearly twenty-four hours. He calls next for his notes on his autobiography and his diary. After again repulsing Hedwig, this time calling her an interloper, he goes into the parlor with Gina to assemble his papers. Hedwig quickly takes up the pistol and disappears into the attic.

Hialmar comes back into the parlor, exhausted from his strenuous efforts at packing. He automatically reaches for the coffee and bread and butter, while he declaims on how he and his father will go out into the snow from home to home seeking shelter. But since he has lost his hat, he must wait until another can be found. He looks about on the tray for more butter. As Gina brings it to him, he eats more buttered bread while he pastes together old Werle's letter that he tore up the day before. He agrees to stay for a day or two in the parlor while he finishes preparations for his departure.

Gregers returns and encourages Hialmar with suggestions that Hedwig may yet make a free-will offering for his sake. Young Ekdal laments the duplicity of Gina and the cruelty of his supposed daughter, who probably never really returned his indescribably great love for her.

They hear a shot from the attic. Hialmar and Gina rush to the attic, where Hedwig lies upon the floor. They carry her in, calling for Doctor Relling. There is nothing he can do for her; death was instantaneous. Hialmar calls upon the heavens: "Why hast thou done this to me?" After he and Gina carry the body out, Gregers insists that young Ekdal's soul will now be liberated and ennobled. Relling caustically replies that within a year Hedwig will mean nothing more to Hialmar than a pretty topic to orate about, with the usual sentimentality and self-pity. Gregers says that if Relling is right then life is not worth living. His destiny, so he tells the Doctor, is to be the thirteenth at table.

Comment

The principal **theme** of the play is stated at the beginning of this act, after Relling attempts to open Gregers' eyes as to what sort of man Hialmar really is. Young Werle admits that he can only fulfill his "claim of the ideal" outside himself. Gregers is thus the opposite of Brand, who sought his demand of the ideal within himself and found it in his final sacrifice. Young Werle, on the other hand, is only able to sacrifice others. Relling then remarks on how essential the "life-lie" is to a man. Hialmar's greatest life-lie is his invention. Even Gregers, who insists on ideal truth, has a life-lie; his blind admiration of his former schoolmate Hialmar. What Ibsen suggests at this point is that the ideal truth which Gregers Werle strives for, as did Doctor Stockmann and Brand, is not always beneficial but often dangerous. Men need their little illusions in order to adjust to their lives.

Hialmar's conduct during this act leaves no doubt about his character. He builds up a little melodrama, turning Hedwig away and preparing to leave forever. His self-pity can be seen in the melancholy picture he draws of himself and his father looking for shelter in the storm. The lack of a hat settles that matter, since Hialmar is averse to taking unnecessary risks. All the time he talks about leaving, he drinks coffee and eats bread and butter and even asks for more butter. His pasting together the letter is almost a stroke of genius on Ibsen's part.

Dramatic **irony** is evident when Gregers tells Hialmar that Hedwig may make a sacrifice for her father's sake. The sacrifice she finally makes is not what Gregers is thinking of. Also ironic is Hialmar's remark about his great love for Hedwig. By now it is fairly obvious that the only person he ever really loved is himself. At the end of the play we see more evidence of his selfishness when he asks why this was done to him.

Gregers' final lines suggest either that he contemplates suicide or that he now finally realizes he is a superfluous person, the thirteenth at table. Ibsen gives us no definite clue, but Gregers' earlier refusal of money from his father was motivated by his feeling no need for it, since what little he has will last his time.

The ending of this play would be tragic if it were not for the focus on Hialmar's selfish posing. Ibsen thus maintains the comic spirit over the tragic, but the comic spirit is rather sardonic, especially when Relling is the spokesman as he is at the end.

THE WILD DUCK

CHARACTER ANALYSES

GREGERS WERLE

Gregers Werle is an impractical idealist whose sole concern is to present his "claim of the ideal." This urge manifests itself in a desire to place the Ekdals' marriage on a firm basis of fact. He idolizes Hialmar Ekdal, whom he considers graced with a noble soul and a high mind. Ibsen gives us some explanation of Gregers' neurosis. The young man was raised by his mother to hate his father. The sympathy he feels for Hialmar may in part be due to the latter's having been raised by two maiden aunts.

HIALMAR EKDAL

Hialmar Ekdal is a true cousin of Peer Gynt, quite happy to loll about the studio while his ego is fed by his wife and daughter as well as by the admiring Gregers. Young Ekdal likes the sound of his own voice and incessantly moralizes on his position as worker, breadwinner, and future inventor, none of which he has ever been or is ever likely to be. He inclines toward the spectacular, and enjoys creating little scenes of which he is the center. As we learn from Doctor Relling, Hialmar was brought up to be admired as the center of attraction.

GINA

Gina, his wife, is basically a sound, steady type, despite her past affair with Werle Senior. Her bad grammar and inept choice of words display her lack of education, yet she keeps the Ekdal household together by feeding her husband's stomach as well as his ego, while at the same time she takes care of the family business.

HEDWIG

Hedwig, the Ekdals' daughter, is the only true idealist in the play, since she alone is willing to make a sacrifice for others. Her near-blindness, like that of her probable real father, Werle Senior, is symbolic. This defect may be taken as representing the unseeing lives of the Ekdals, happy in their own life-lies or illusions, just as old Werle's poor eyesight is indicative of his moral blindness.

OLD WERLE

Old Werle is reminiscent both of Consul Bernick (*Pillars of Society*) and Chamberlain Alving (*Ghosts*). A former libertine, he is equally unscrupulous in business. Old Ekdal went to jail in his place as a result of one of his illegal business deals. Werle salves his conscience by paying the broken old man a high price for the little copying he does.

DOCTOR RELLING AND MOLVIK

Doctor Relling and Molvik are two examples of social wreckage, like Krogstad in *A Doll's House*. The Doctor, however, despite the ruin he made of his own life, is still intelligent, and, like Doctor Stockmann (*An Enemy of the People*), is Ibsen's own mouthpiece at times. Ibsen attempts without much success to give added dimension to Relling's character by alluding to an earlier attachment with Mrs. Sorby.

HEDDA GABLER

INTRODUCTION

Beginning with *The Wild Duck* (1884), Ibsen turned away from dramas of social significance to devote his energies to psychological analyses of character. His next two plays, *Rosmersholm* (1886) and *The Lady from the Sea* (1888), are thus more concerned with inner emotional conflicts than with social or political themes. Like *The Wild Duck*, both of these plays afford penetrating analyses of character in Ibsen's usual fashion of disclosing past facts, one by one, that have contributed to the formation of character. Both plays are also comparable to their predecessor in the emphasis placed on symbolism, which is so complex that the plays are difficult to interpret.

In *Hedda Gabler*, however, Ibsen returned for the last time to the realistic technique of the great social plays. The play is written with almost complete objectivity. Symbolism is absent, except for Hedda's thin hair and her pistols, and the recurrent phrase "vine leaves in his hair." But these are so transparent compared to the white horses and the sea in *Rosmersholm*, or to the wild duck, that they hardly qualify as symbols. Some critics prefer to regard them simply as marks of character.

Although the major emphasis in *Hedda Gabler* is on intimate psychological analysis, it is not hard to find at least some social significance. Hedda represents an emancipated woman who, like Mrs. Alving in *Ghosts*, finds herself with a great deal of intellectual freedom, yet with emotions that have failed to keep pace in their development. Hedda, then, is left without any outlets for her emotions, which appear almost dried up. Accordingly she has no opportunity ever to find herself, to come to any understanding of herself, as Mrs. Alving does when she realizes the extent to which her "ghosts" have ruled her, or as *Peer Gynt* does, when he finally sees what his life and his love really were. The characterization of Hedda may be regarded as a study of the effects of the new emancipation upon women. This conclusion is supported by the fact that Ibsen patterned Hedda's character after an eighteen-year-old Austrian, Emilie Bardach, who intended to devote her life to taking married men away from their wives. In 1889, Ibsen was captivated by her for a brief time. He kept up a lively and sometimes passionate correspondence, but he soon terminated their friendship and settled down to an objective study of her. The result was *Hedda Gabler* (1890).

CHARACTERS

George Tesman, a scholar.

Hedda Tesman, his wife.

Miss Juliana Tesman, his aunt.

Mrs. Thea Elvsted, a former schoolgirl with Hedda, and at one time a friend of George.

Judge Brack, a friend of the Tesmans.

Eilert Lovborg, a brilliant but alcoholic scholar, formerly a friend of Hedda and George.

Berta, the Tesmans' servant.

The setting is the drawing room of the Tesmans' villa in Christiania (now Oslo), Norway.

HEDDA GABLER

TEXTUAL ANALYSIS

ACT ONE

Act One (morning). The play opens with a conversation between Juliana, Tesman's aunt, and Berta, their servant. In this rather conventional way, Ibsen presents his **exposition** or background information. George and Hedda have just returned from a six-month wedding tour through Europe, during which he received a doctorate. He enters, happy to see his aunt again. He inquires after Rina, her invalid sister, and remarks on the gorgeous new bonnet Aunt Juliana is wearing. She is anxious to discover if Hedda is pregnant, but George takes her hints about an increase in the household to refer to his library. He is shocked to find out that his aunts have mortgaged their annuity to pay for the new house and furnishings. Aunt Juliana is hopeful for his prospects, since his greatest rival for the professorship he expects is the disreputable Eilert Lovborg, who has been away for years.

Hedda comes in, complaining first of the excessive sunshine and fresh air, then of the servant's old bonnet on a chair. Juliana is insulted at this reference to her new hat, but she hides her feelings. Hedda vigorously denies any suggestion that she might be pregnant.

When George asks that his wife use the familiar du rather than the formal de in addressing Aunt Juliana, Hedda refuses, but she does agree to call her "Aunt." Hedda then notices that her old piano does not fit the room arrangement. She suggests keeping it in the inner room and buying another for the drawing room.

Mrs. Thea Elvsted comes in, and tells about her marriage to Sheriff Elvsted and her stepchildren, to whom Eilert Lovborg had been appointed tutor. While George goes within to write a letter to Lovborg, Mrs. Elvsted tells Hedda how she has been helping Eilert for the last two years with his books. She tells Hedda of his memory of a woman whom he is unable to forget, one who threatened to shoot him with a pistol when they parted. Hedda comments coldly: "No one does that sort of thing here." Mrs. Elvsted thinks that it probably was a red-headed singer who, she hears, is in town again.

Judge Brack arrives to inform George that his appointment as professor may be made contingent upon a competition with Lovborg. George is indignant and greatly concerned, while Hedda says she is "most eager to see who wins." After the Judge leaves, George is very worried about his financial prospects, while Hedda is only upset because she cannot keep open house and have the liveried footman and saddle-horses she was promised. She retires into the inner room to play with her pistols, which formerly belonged to General Gabler, her father.

Comment

The characters of George and Hedda are particularly well delineated in this act. George is sufficiently involved in his work to take his aunt's hints as meaning his library. He also remarks on the quantity of notes he was able to take during their wedding trip. It is easy to envision George and Hedda spending their honeymoon going from one library to another.

Hedda's neurotic disposition is clear in the **episode** over the bonnet. As she confides to Brack in the second act, she only pretended to think it was the servant's hat. Hedda's urge to injure motivates the greater part of her conversation with her husband. Her whole attitude is one of condescending tolerance, and her caustic remarks could only go unnoticed by a man like George Tesman. The manner in which she repulses Aunt Juliana's attentions and then practically forces herself upon Mrs. Elvsted shows her intensely and completely selfish nature. George's aunt means nothing to her, but Mrs. Elvsted is a possible source of information about Lovborg. The references to Hedda's thin hair and Thea Elvsted's abundant blond hair are very significant. Ibsen suggests that their capacities for life and love are matched by their hair. Hedda with her thin hair is emotionally and spiritually arid, although intellectually and socially brilliant: Thea Elvsted, although a little inclined towards stupidity, leaves her husband to follow Lovborg mainly because of her comparatively greater emotional capacity, which was unfulfilled in her loveless marriage to the Sheriff.

Thea's reference to the lady with the pistols and Hedda's comment pave the way for the conclusion of the play, as does Hedda's leaving to play with her pistols at the end of the act. Another and more subtle example of this sort of dramatic preparation is George's persistent mistake in referring to Thea Elvsted by her maiden name, Miss Rysing. It anticipates the budding partnership between the two at the end of the play.

Hedda's utter lack of sympathy for George's dismay over the competition for the professorship as well as her bitter disappointment over their financial restrictions are clear proof that the marriage was one of convenience only.

HEDDA GABLER

TEXTUAL ANALYSIS

ACT TWO

Act Two (afternoon). Hedda stands by the door, loading a pistol. She points it into the air and fires it over the head of the approaching Judge Brack. Annoyed and not a little frightened, he takes the pistol from her and puts it back in its case. They have a confidential talk in which she reviews the boredom of her honeymoon. When asked why she chose Tesman whom she admits she does not love, she answers that "her day was done," and he seemed a likely prospect.

Brack makes it clear that he is interested in a "triangular friendship." Hedda shows little enthusiasm. Tesman's arrival turns their attention to him. Hedda's sarcasm is as usual lost upon him, as when he announces that Aunt Juliana will not be able to come because of her sister's illness. Hedda's answer is "I must bear my disappointment."

She then explains the bonnet incident, and confesses to Brack that such impulses come over her suddenly and she finds them irresistible. She complains as always of boredom, and the Judge suggests motherhood. The very thought sickens her. She says there is only one thing she is fit for: boring herself to death.

First George and then Lovborg come in. The latter tells of his new book dealing with the future. When George, amazed, says he never thought of writing such a thing, Hedda comments audibly, "Hmm... I daresay not." Lovborg tells Tesman that he will not contest the professorship, but will deliver a series of lectures later, to secure only a "moral victory" over his rival. Tesman goes into the inner room to drink with Brack while Lovborg and Hedda remain.

The two were at one time close friends, but Hedda claims that for her it was largely the thrill of doing something in secret, having a friendship that no one suspected. She admits that she broke off their friendship when Eilert threatened to become serious. Her emotions almost betray her for a moment when she states that her not shooting him down as she had threatened was not her most cowardly act that evening long before. But any further talk is interrupted by Mrs. Elvsted's arrival.

Hedda then attempts to make Lovborg drink punch, over Thea's objection. She finally succeeds in getting Eilert to drink, then encourages him to attend Brack's party, despite Thea's remonstrances. As the act ends, Hedda claims that Eilert will return as he promised at ten, with vine leaves in his hair.

Comment

Hedda's obvious ability to shoot is another example of dramatic preparation, since Hedda later lends one pistol to Lovborg and shoots herself with the other. Her dialogues with Brack reveal her apparent incapability of feeling deep emotions. She is disgusted by the word "love," and knowledge of her own pregnancy, which George and Aunt Juliana already suspect, makes the thought of motherhood repellent to her. Hedda's boredom is the result of her inability or complete unwillingness to commit herself emotionally to anyone or anything. It is symptomatic of a pathologically self-centered nature.

Hedda's earlier friendship again suggests her fear of emotional commitment. Her affair with Lovborg was never anything more than a Platonic relationship, devoid of anything sensual. When it did promise to become "serious," then Hedda threatened him with her pistols. These pistols are thus Hedda's symbolic weapon against the external world; when it threatens to encroach upon her personal boredom, she takes the pistols out and fires them, as she does in the direction of Brack, whose intentions are not acceptable to her even if his conversation is.

The reference to "vine leaves in his hair" of course refers to a manner of self-decoration common in classic times, particularly in the worship of the Greek god of wine, Dionysus, and his Roman counterpart Bacchus. For an interesting if rather forced reading of *Hedda Gabler's* character as "Dionysiac," the reader should refer to G. Wilson Knight's *Henrik Ibsen*, pp. 62-67 (see Bibliography). The chief significance for us is that Hedda is looking for Eilert to do something beautiful, noble, and great, to her and through her help. We are reminded at this point of Gregers Werle in *The Wild Duck*, who also was compelled by his own spiritual aridity to seek his ideal outside himself. Another significance of this phrase is that Hedda, by so insisting on Eilert's performance, betrays a well-concealed depth of emotion in herself. Her taut, over-restrained feelings also show in her nervous habits, clenching her hands, rapping on windowpanes, etc. The most obvious betrayal of these inner feelings was her momentary lapse when she told Lovborg that her greatest cowardice years ago was not in failing to shoot him. Her meaning is that it was more cowardly of her to send him away, thus rejecting her own feeling for him.

Hedda's sending Eilert off to the party despite the danger of a relapse into his former alcoholism cannot be interpreted as anything beautiful, although she insists on his returning with vine leaves. Her motives are mixed. On the surface, she is torn by jealousy of Thea Elvsted, who is able to inspire Lovborg to write great books. A more subtle motive, however, is connected with her irresistible urges, as in the bonnet incident, to do injury. These feelings, which in the case of Lovborg may be in effect urges to hurt a loved one, have a basis in her emotional and sexual frigidity. Although she seems to have feelings deep within, she is incapable of expressing them, and horrified by the thought of their development into anything more substantial. In a word, she is afraid of sex when it involves emotion, and only disgusted with it when emotion is not present, as with Tesman.

HEDDA GABLER

TEXTUAL ANALYSIS

ACT THREE

Act Three (early the next morning). Hedda and Mrs. Elvsted have been waiting all night for the return of George and Eilert. Hedda, who has just awakened from her sleep on the couch, tells Mrs. Elvsted that there is nothing to worry about, and insists that she go off to get a little rest. A letter comes from Juliana.

George enters and tells Hedda about how Eilert became drunk and lost his manuscript which he found by the side of the road. He did not return it immediately because Eilert was too drunk. George is unable to conceal his jealousy of the new book, and at the same time, worried about having the manuscript in his possession, he tells Hedda that no one must know.

George then sees the letter from Aunt Juliana and from it learns that her sister is dying. While the upset and confused George tries to put on his gloves, Hedda seizes the manuscript. As he leaves, she promises to keep it until he returns.

Judge Brack then comes in to tell Hedda about what really happened during the night. Eilert eventually landed in the apartment of Mademoiselle Diana, the red-haired singer whom Mrs. Elvsted mentioned in the first act. Missing his pocketbook and his manuscript, he accused her or her friends of robbery. In the fight that resulted, Lovborg struck one of the police officers who came to quiet the group. Brack makes it very plain to Hedda that no respectable house, including hers of course, will receive Lovborg as a guest. The Judge makes it equally clear that he will tolerate no competition from Eilert or anyone else in the comfortable triangle he is trying to arrange. Hedda sees through his polite words and merely laughs.

Lovborg enters and is greeted by Hedda and then by Mrs. Elvsted. He repulses the latter by telling her he has destroyed the manuscript. She compares his act with child-murder, then leaves in despair. Lovborg confesses to Hedda that he has simply lost the manuscript, but he did not have the courage to admit that to Mrs. Elvsted, for losing their "child" in such a fashion is even worse than destroying it. He is determined to end his life, and Hedda gives him one of her pistols, insisting that he do it beautifully. After he leaves, Hedda goes to the stove and burns the manuscript, piece by piece, saying that she is burning the child of Eilert and "curly-locks," her name for Mrs. Elvsted, of whose hair she has always been jealous.

Comment

George's state of mind when he enters with Lovborg's manuscript is not difficult to perceive. He cannot help admitting to Hedda his jealousy of Eilert's talent. His delay in returning the manuscript and his decision not to tell anyone, even Lovborg, suggest that he himself is not quite sure why he brought it home or what he intends to do with it.

Brack's motives are very obvious. He insists that he will be the only "cock-in-the-basket," and to assure his comfortable arrangement with Hedda and George, he will remove any possible intruders. Hence he is interested enough in Lovborg's doings to get him drunk at the party and then afterward find out what he did. Brack's designs upon Hedda are quite evident, and she fully realizes what he wants when she tells him that she is glad he has no hold over her.

Hedda's destroying of the manuscript is prompted largely by Thea Elvsted's and then Lovborg's reference to the manuscript as their child. Hedda cannot bear the thought that anyone could have more power to inspire Lovborg than she herself. Therefore she first gives him a pistol to shoot himself, then destroys the last evidence of his relationship with Mrs. Elvsted.

HEDDA GABLER

TEXTUAL ANALYSIS

ACT FOUR

Act Four (evening of the same day). Dressed in mourning clothes, Aunt Juliana brings the news of her sister's death to George and to Hedda, who is also dressed in black. He and his aunt again suspect Hedda's pregnancy, a subject which as usual Hedda brusquely evades. George asks Hedda for the manuscript. She refuses, then confesses that she has burned it. Her shocked husband can only exclaim that she has been guilty of "illegal appropriation of lost property." Hedda then declares that she has done it for his sake, and then indirectly admits her pregnancy. In this scene she for the first time calls him by his first name, George. He is so happy that he nearly forgets all about the manuscript.

Mrs. Elvsted enters hastily, fearful that something has happened to Lovborg. Her alarm is soon confirmed by Judge Brack, who brings news of Eilert. The latter shot himself and is now in the hospital. George and Mrs. Elvsted are horrified, but Hedda considers Lovborg's action beautiful and courageous. George is dismayed that both Eilert and his book are destroyed. At this moment Mrs. Elvsted produces a packet of notes from which Lovborg had dictated his book. She and George retire to the inner room to study and arrange the papers.

Brack then informs Hedda of the truth about Lovborg, who first of all is already dead, and secondly, was found shot in Mademoiselle Diana's bedroom. To complete Hedda's confusion, Brack reveals that Lovborg was not shot in the breast, as the Judge said earlier, but in the intestine. Hedda then despairingly asks what curse makes everything she touches "turn ludicrous and mean." The Judge then informs Hedda that the pistol found on Lovborg must have been stolen. Hedda denies it.

At this moment George and Mrs. Elvsted return from the inner room. Needing more room and better light they set themselves up at Hedda's writing table, but first Hedda brings some sheet music and an object concealed under it into the inner room. George goes about his task happily, exclaiming that "arranging other people's papers" is the work he is best at.

Brack then continues to apply pressure on Hedda. He warns her of the great danger of scandal she is now in, but he promises to protect her, at a price. The price is to be her surrender to him. Hedda cannot endure the idea of being in Brack's power. When he answers that people become accustomed to the inevitable, Hedda's reply is a simple but dramatic "Yes, perhaps."

Imitating George's way of speech, Hedda asks him how he is getting on. She passes her hands through Thea Elvsted's hair, commenting on how Thea is now working with George the way she used to with Eilert. She asks if there is anything she can do to help the two of them. George answers in the negative.

Hedda goes into the inner room and plays a wild dance on the piano. George asks her to stop and to think of Aunt Rina and

Eilert Lovborg. Hedda thrusts her head through the curtains screening the inner room and cries out "And of Aunt Juliana. And of all the rest ... After this I will be silent."

George then suggests to Mrs. Elvsted that she stay at Aunt Juliana's, where he and she can devote their evenings to reconstructing Eilert's book. When Hedda calls out to ask what she will do in the evenings, George mentions that Judge Brack will be kind enough to visit her then. A shot is heard from within. George draws aside the curtains, to see Hedda lying dead on the couch. As the curtain drops Judge Brack cries out, "Good God! People don't do such things."

Comment

At the beginning of the act Hedda is dressed in black, which represents her mourning for Eilert, who she hopes is to die beautifully. George's reaction when she admits burning the manuscript is particularly enlightening. He betrays himself not really as grief-stricken as perhaps he should be. His feelings are tinged slightly with joy, so that his happiness overflows when Hedda implies that she is pregnant.

Mrs. Elvsted's sudden production of Lovborg's notes is one of the more obvious faults in the plot of *Hedda Gabler*. It is extremely unlikely that any woman in her situation would carry a large package of notes everywhere she goes.

Hedda's quest for something beautiful, earlier symbolized by the phrase "vine leaves in his hair," now is concentrated in desire to learn of Lovborg's beautiful death. That his death can seem so lovely to her now is a clear indication of where her own thoughts for herself are beginning to turn, as is her inability to

refrain from comments upon his death even in front of George and Brack. Her realization that she has ruined everything she has turned to is a sign that she is now even more aware of the frustration and uselessness of her life, where before she complained only of boredom. When she smuggles the pistol into the inner room, it is obvious that she contemplates suicide.

The end of the play presents a powerful scene in which Hedda seems to make one futile bid for acceptance. She refuses Brack's offer of a genteel adultery and her answer to the Judge's remark on its being inevitable is ironic, since she has already been contemplating what now seems even more inevitable, her own death.

The ease with which George and Mrs. Elvsted work together arouses Hedda's jealousy, which she controls with great effort while she strokes Thea Elvsted's hair, the hair she had years ago at school once threatened to burn. When she is told she can be of no help, she perhaps further realizes her loneliness.

Hedda's long pent-up emotions burst forth in the wild dance she plays on the piano. Her answer, that after this she will be silent, is another example of dramatic **irony**, since she plans the total silence of death.

The final motive for Hedda's suicide comes with George's simple suggestion that Judge Brack entertain her in the evenings. Unable to face Brack now that he has "a hold" over her, she ends her life. The Judge's final comment is typical of his thoroughly conventional outlook, but it also recalls Hedda's comment to Mrs. Elvsted in the first act, when the latter mentions an unknown woman who once threatened Eilert Lovborg with a pistol. Hedda replies, "No one does that sort of thing here." Hedda Gabler was thus just as much a slave of **convention** as Judge Brack.

HEDDA GABLER

CHARACTERS ANALYSES

HEDDA GABLER

Hedda Gabler is an extremely neurotic woman. Intellectually she is brilliant compared to her husband, whom she treats with thinly veiled contempt. Her upbringing as General Gabler's daughter prepared her for a life of bright, gay social entertainment which as the wife of a scholar she cannot afford. Partly because of this upbringing, she has gradually developed into a coldhearted, perverse woman, utterly incapable of showing affection for anyone. So disciplined are her emotions that she can no longer entertain any affection for a former friend, Eilert Lovborg. What should have been love in Hedda becomes a passion to see him do something she would consider beautiful. But her idea of beauty, like her own character, is perverted. His death, if done nobly, would seem beautiful to her. This concentration upon death, first Eilert's and then her own, is indicative of the spiritual emptiness of Hedda Gabler. In reassessing herself, as she seems to do after Eilert's unlovely death, she catches a glimpse of her own emptiness and purposelessness. Her suicide is then almost inevitable.

Despite her' external coldness, Hedda does have a potentiality for feeling. But her emotions have been suppressed for so long that they can only display themselves in grotesquely altered forms. Hence she is satanically jealous of The as Elvsted, contemptuous of her husband, occasionally abusive to Aunt Juliana, and not very careful with her toys, the pistols.

Finally, whatever emotion she feels toward Eilert is expressed in the destruction of the manuscript, a symbol of his relationship with another woman, and in her wish for his death. All of these expressions of emotion are in the form of irresistible urges, as for example, her final wild piano-playing just before her death. Her suicide may be viewed as the final manifestation of a deep-seated death wish (intense longing for self-destruction), which is symbolized by her playing with her pistols.

Like many neurotic women, Hedda is intensely self-centered. Lovborg, for example, is important to her only in that she might be able to influence him to do something beautiful for her. His death affects her only in so far as it gives her a feeling of liberation to know that something meeting her twisted standards of beauty can occur.

GEORGE TESMAN

George Tesman is a caricature (exaggerated comic portrait) of a scholar. His intellect is well adapted to what he calls his "special subjects," but he is no match for Hedda's subtlety. He spent his honeymoon collecting research materials for his projected history of the domestic industries of Brabant in the Middle Ages. His days are spent in reading, studying and writing, whereas his wife would prefer brilliant entertainments and sparkling conversations. George Tesman is far too conventional and stodgy to participate in either. His favorite expression, "Fancy that!" is a good example of his conversational ability, and is indicative of his completely colorless personality.

EILERT LOVBORG

Eilert Lovborg is a less successful characterization. He belongs to a personality-type which Ibsen has already thoroughly explored; he is representative of the social wreckage in earlier plays, such as Krogstad in *A Doll's House*, and Relling in *The Wild Duck*. His motive for destroying himself by returning to drink is rather conventionally melodramatic. He feels that Thea Elvsted by following him has shown lack of faith in his reformation, and, goaded by Hedda, he proves that Thea was right. He affords good contrast to George Tesman, for while the latter is conventional and talented, Lovborg is unconventional and inspired.

THEA ELVSTED

Thea Elvsted is a foil or contrasting character to Hedda. She has abundant blond hair of which Hedda is wildly jealous. The hair symbolizes Mrs. Elvsted's capacity for emotion and for partaking fully of life, while Hedda's thin hair reflects her own emotional aridity.

THE MASTER BUILDER

INTRODUCTION

In 1892, two years after *Hedda Gabler*, Ibsen returned to the experimentation with symbolism that marked the preceding two plays, *Rosmersholm* (1886) and *The Lady from the Sea* (1888). The symbolism in *The Master Builder* is complex and sometimes vague, but it is possible to extract an autobiographical interpretation. Accordingly, the churches which Solness builds at the beginning of his career represent Ibsen's romantic plays, particularly *Brand* (1866). The "homes for human beings" to which Solness next turns correspond to the dramatist's social plays (1877 to 1882), and the "castles in the air" that Solness finally conceives represent Ibsen's symbolic and spiritual dramas starting with *Rosmersholm*. The problem with such an autobiographical reading is that there is no evidence to carry the similarity between Solness and Ibsen much further. It is true that Ibsen may have been dissatisfied with his accomplishments to date just as Solness is. Not even the youthful Austrian femme fatale Emilie Bardach, already mentioned in connection with *Hedda Gabler*, had any impact on Ibsen comparable to that of Hilda Wangel on Solness. Furthermore, if the dramatist's marriage was by 1892 in the same sorry state as Solness', the Ibsens were very careful to conceal the matter from the world at large as well as from their friends. There are, of course, a few lesser parallels between Solness' career and Ibsen's, and these will be noted in the following analysis.

The Master Builder may be compared with *Brand*. Both plays involve the tragedy of men whose ideals are set too high. But there is a wide difference between Brand's personal "demand of the ideal," his insistence upon "all or nothing," and the driving ambition of Solness which leads him to exploit ruthlessly his own wife, the Brovicks, and their niece Kaia. Whereas Brand is altruistic in seeking to raise himself and all mankind to a higher level, Solness seems more self-centered in his drive to gain fame through his buildings.

CHARACTERS

Halvard Solness, Master Builder.

Aline Solness, his wife.

Doctor Herdal, physician.

Knut Brovick, a former architect, now employed by Solness.

Ragnar Brovick, his son, a draftsman.

Kaia Fosli (pronounced Kye-uh), Brovick's niece and bookkeeper for Solness.

Miss Hilda Wangel, daughter of the district doctor at Lysanger.

Ladies, Crowd, etc.

The setting is in and around the Solness home.

THE MASTER BUILDER

TEXTUAL ANALYSIS

ACT ONE

In his office Solness speaks to Kaia, who is obviously in love with him. From the next room, Ragnar Brovick tells him that a young couple interested in having a home built are anxious to see their plans. Solness is impatient and swears that he would rather give up the commission that be rushed.

Old Brovick, who is very ill, then asks Solness if he would step aside and allow Ragnar to design and build the house. Solness angrily refuses to "give way to anybody." Before he passes on, Brovick wants to see Ragnar succeed, but Solness is firm. He apologizes defiantly: "I am what I am, and I cannot change my nature."

Solness then tells Kaia, over whom he seems to have a great deal of influence, to marry Ragnar and talk him into staying with the Master Builder. Mrs. Solness breaks in on them quietly, making her jealousy of her husband apparent but unobtrusive.

Doctor Herdal and Solness then discuss Mrs. Solness' jealousy, and the Doctor asks if there is any justification for her attitude. Solness tells him that Kaia Fosli is in love with him, but he is not in love with her. He has never told his wife the truth, because he feels by doing him an injustice she is helping him to pay a huge debt he owes to her.

Solness then accuses the Doctor of plotting with his wife. He is sure that they both think he is insane. When the Doctor vigorously denies the charge, Solness explains why he is not really the happy man people consider him to be. The burning down of Solness' first home was a blow from which Aline never recovered, even though it became lucky for Solness himself. The latter then goes on to explain to the Doctor how he fears the younger generation which any moment may knock at his door, and then his end will come.

A knock is heard at the door, and Hilda Wangel enters, a delicately built young lady, in shortened skirt and sailor shirt and hat, with a knapsack on her back. She asks to stay a few nights, and Mrs. Solness, who met her at a sanatarium, agrees. She is given one of the three nurseries. The Solnesses have no children but their home has three furnished nurseries.

Hilda then reminds Solness of what he has forgotten. She tells him how they first met ten years ago to the day, when she was a schoolgirl of twelve watching him place a wreath high on the top of a church steeple in the little town of Lysanger. The experience was extremely thrilling for Hilda, who waved a flag and screamed so much that he became dizzy and almost fell. Solness remembers the incident, but of what Hilda next tells he recalls nothing. Miss Wangel then describes how at a reception later that same day at her father's house Solness and she were alone. He told her she would be his princess when she grew up, and he promised that in ten years he would come like a troll to carry her off to Spain and buy her a kingdom. Hilda has now come at the end of ten years to collect her kingdom. Solness now feels that her coming is good for him. Up to now he has feared the younger generation. Now he sees "youth lined up against youth," that is, Hilda will be on his side.

Comment

The huge debt which Solness feels that he owes his wife is only partly explained in the first act. In the next act we shall learn of the loss of their children shortly after the fire, and of Mrs. Solness' broken health ever since. Solness has a guilty conscience about the matter, and of this, too, more will be said later. Ibsen, as usual, unfolds gradually the past experiences that have shaped his characters.

Solness' accusation of Doctor Herdal clearly shows that the Master Builder has been worried about his own mental state. His sudden accusation and his conviction that his wife and the Doctor are conspiring against him are evidence of Solness' paranoia (a mental state characterized by systematic delusions of persecution or grandeur).

The arrival of Hilda right after Solness' reference to the younger generation's knocking at his door is an example of **foreshadowing**. Although Solness is unaware of his danger, Hilda will bring about his destruction.

Hilda Wangel is one of Ibsen's most elusive characters. She might be explained as a young woman whose greatest emotional experience so far has been her vision of Solness climbing the heights, and now she has come to recapture that experience. For a lengthy and detailed psychoanalysis of Hilda from this point of view, the reader should consult Herman J. Weigand, *The Modern Ibsen*, pp. 288-299 (see Bibliography). But beyond the psychological level, Hilda has definite symbolic meaning in this play. She is, as it were, the projection of Solness' desire to prolong his youth and to continue in his work, building higher and higher monuments to his own glory. In the action of the play, she is the energizing force that impels Solness to his last and fatal attempt to aspire to the heights.

THE MASTER BUILDER

TEXTUAL ANALYSIS

ACT TWO

In the drawing room, Solness tells his wife that she will find it much easier in their new home. She laments that he will never again be able to build a real home for her. She still grieves for the death of their "little ones" shortly after the burning of their home years before. Solness alludes to his madness, then to his debt to her, both of which mystify his wife. Hilda enters, and Mrs. Solness leaves, saying that it is her duty to get her some extra clothes to wear. Hilda comments on the cold, comfortless word "duty."

Solness points out the new house and tower he has built next to their present home. When Hilda asks if it also will have three nurseries, Solness explains how their twin boys died shortly after the fire. After their death, he no longer desired to build churches, the one at Lysanger, Hilda's town, being his last one. After that he turned to building "homes for human beings." The destruction of their house proved to be lucky for him, since he built a number of homes on its extensive grounds, thereby making his reputation and his fortune.

Solness then confesses to Hilda his guilty feelings about the fire, since he had wished their old home to burn down, and had even neglected a crack in the chimney, hoping that the house would burn. At this point, Ragnar Brovick enters and asks for Solness' approval of his plans. Solness refuses and insists that Ragnar stay with him. Hilda is disappointed at the mean and base treatment of the younger Brovick.

Solness then continues to explain his guilty feelings about the fire. He believes that he has unusual power of wishing a thing into existence, and that the secret of these powers lies in certain supernatural beings he calls "helpers" and "servants." Hilda calls it the "troll" in him, and looks upon his guilty feelings as manifestations of a "sickly conscience." Her own conscience is robust and healthy, like the conscience of an ancient Viking, a comparison which Solness explicitly makes. He likens Hilda to a bird of prey and to the sunrise. She is the younger generation of which he used to be afraid.

Hilda then insists that he approve Ragnar's plans and she sees that he does. Kaia Fosli is then sent to bring the plans to Ragnar, and also to bring the news that both she and Ragnar are dismissed from Solness' employ. Now that Hilda's idol has just done a noble deed, she is eager to see him climb up to the high tower of his new house to hang the wreath. Mrs. Solness is shocked, because her husband cannot stand heights. To Hilda, it will simply be a great trill.

Comment

Mrs. Solness' stress on duty is reminiscent of *Ghosts*, in which Mrs. Alving's earlier years were devoted to a cold, stern approach to duty. Yet the picture Solness gives of his wife Aline before the tragedy is of joyous young motherhood.

Solness' decision to direct his attention away from churches and devote his time to building homes parallels Ibsen's own shift from romantic plays to realistic social dramas. In the context of the play, however, Solness, action signifies a rejection of church and of God that approaches defiance. His motivation is further developed in the next act.

The reason for Solness' conviction that he owes a great debt to his wife is his feeling that he has sacrificed her entire life for his art, for his buildings. He has destroyed Aline Solness' life in making a worldly success of his own.

Solness' refusal to help Ragnar is due to his own need for the Brovicks, who are trained architects. By his own admission, Solness is a builder, not an architect, because he lacks the training. Thus the Master Builder is here doubly selfish, because he is moved not only by fear of a possible rival but even more by his need for the Brovicks' talents.

Solness is unable to climb heights because of his vertigo (susceptibility to dizzy spells). But Hilda insists upon his repeating his thrilling exploit of ten years before, and he agrees. The practice of hanging a wreath upon the top of a new building was a common Scandinavian custom.

THE MASTER BUILDER

TEXTUAL ANALYSIS

ACT THREE

Hilda and Mrs. Solness are on the veranda of the Solness home. Mrs. Solness tells her about the burning of their house and the loss of the twins, but she is not as affected by either loss now as she is by the destruction of all her things. All of the furnishings, clothing, lace, and the jewelry that link her to the past are gone, and, above all, her nine dolls that she treasured were all destroyed.

Mrs. Solness goes off to speak to Doctor Herdal about her husband. Hilda then tells Solness how she has just felt a chill-a reference to Mrs. Solness. Hilda has decided to leave, because she cannot take Solness away from his wife. She asks what he will build next. Since he is undecided, she suggests the "loveliest thing in the world," which turns out to be "castles in the air."

Ragnar brings the wreath for the top of the tower, and then remains to watch the festivities. He talks to Hilda about Kaia, who confessed to him that Solness "had taken possession of ...

her whole mind." Hilda can scarcely conceal her jealousy. Ragnar concludes by explaining Solness' infirmity, his dizzy spells that make it impossible for him to climb. Doctor Herdal and Mrs. Solness then come in and ask Hilda to try to convince the Master Builder not to climb the tower.

Solness then explains to Hilda why he is afraid to put the wreath on the tower. He fears not so much his dizziness as punishment from heaven. Years ago at Lysanger when he placed the wreath on the church tower he vowed never again to build a church for the "Mighty One" (God). He decided instead to build homes, but he now realizes that men have no use for these homes and are not happy in them. He has sacrificed his wife and the Brovicks and his own life for nothing, because he has not accomplished anything that satisfied him. He promises Hilda that the two of them will hand and hand build and mount their own castle. She insists first that Kaia be left out. He asks her to believe in him, and she will, provided he climbs the tower once more. He determines to do it.

Solness goes to the new house while everyone waits on the veranda to see the wreath put in position. Ragnar expects to see Solness stay below while another places the wreath, but Hilda insists her Master Builder will climb. Solness is then seen climbing up the scaffolding around the tower. All are alarmed except Hilda, who is again thrilled to see Solness ascend the heights. He falls and is killed. The play ends with Hilda frantically waving her shawl and shrieking, "My Master Builder."

Comment

At the beginning of the act, Mrs. Solness exposes her ultraconservative nature when she asserts that the keenest loss she feels is the loss of her nine dolls. Critics have often objected to Ibsen's presenting a grown woman still cherishing her dolls, but William Archer, Ibsen's first important English translator, wrote in the Westminister Gazette (1893) that a Norwegian cousin of his kept a favorite doll until she was nearly thirty. The dolls symbolize Mrs. Solness' emotional immaturity as well as her conservative nature. Hilda's subsequent reference to the chill she felt in Mrs. Solness' presence testifies to the latter's lifelessness, for as Solness himself confesses he has sacrificed her life to his ambition.

Hilda's jealousy of Kaia evidences the complexity of a character which hitherto has appeared rather simple. At first Hilda seems idealistically conceived, like Solness, as a symbol of greatness and liberation of spirit. Now her jealousy suggests a more feminine motive. But Hilda seems to have no interest in a conventional love affair with Solness; she is fascinated by the anticipation of his once more performing the same thrilling feat that she witnessed at Lysanger.

At the end of the play, Hilda once more undergoes the emotional experience she had at Lysanger. She hears harps and singing, but no one else does. When Solness plunges to his death, she still cries out for her Master Builder. In the plot of this play, Hilda appears as an emotionally unstable and perhaps perverted young lady, whose greatest experience to date has been watching Solness climb the scaffolding. In a symbolic interpretation, Hilda may represent an external agent compelling Solness to further acts of defiance against God.

THE MASTER BUILDER

CHARACTER ANALYSES

HALVARD SOLNESS

Halvard Solness is comparable to Brand in that both are guilty of what the ancient Greeks called hybris (excessive pride or ambition). In his ruthless quest to rise to the top of his profession (symbolized by climbing the tower), he ruins not only his own life, but also the lives of his wife, the two Brovicks, and the young girl Kaia. Solness thus may represent a defiant, inflexible, ambitious man whose career finally ends in tragedy. But he also represents symbolically the position of the creative artist who must, in order to achieve anything, strive to excel, regardless of his own happiness or that of others.

HILDA WANGEL

Hilda Wangel may be interpreted as a neurotic young woman whose emotions, like Hedda Gabler's, have become perverted to the extent that she seeks destruction as a beauty in itself where other women would seek life and love. Also like Hedda Gabler, she is probably patterned after the same real-life femme fatale, Emilie Bardach, with whom Ibsen became briefly involved in 1889. The character of Hilda can also be regarded as symbolic of the defiant ambition of Solness himself. Like Solness, she aspires to "joy of life," but neither of them can find it except in the "castles in the air" which Hilda wants and which he promises her.

MRS. SOLNESS

Mrs. Solness is an extremely conservative woman who lives only for cold, unemotional duty, now that her past has been symbolically destroyed by the fire that took away her family home, her furnishings, and other mementos of her youth. For the loss of their children she assumes the blame, since her insistence on nursing them even during her illness and fever caused their deaths. Like Mrs. Alving in *Ghosts* and Mrs. Rosmer whose shadow falls throughout *Rosmersholm*, she is too much ruled by dead ideas and beliefs to have any of the "joy of life" that both Solness and Hilda aspire to.

PILLARS OF SOCIETY

INTRODUCTION

Pillars of Society is greatly inferior to Ibsen's later plays, but it does show the author's concern for social and moral problems. It ranks as the first and least among Ibsen's social dramas. Written in 1877, it immediately proved very popular on the Continent, but not until the 1890s and later was it performed more than a few scattered times in England and America. The plot of the play follows earlier conventions, for Ibsen devotes more attention to making the piece logically consistent than to rendering it psychologically true.

CHARACTERS

Consul Karsten Bernick, a shipbuilder.

    Mrs. Betty Bernick, his wife.

    Olaf, their son.

    Miss Martha Bernick, the Consul's sister.

Johan Tonnesen, Mrs. Bernick's younger brother.

Miss Lona Hessel, her elder stepsister.

Hilmar Tbnnesen, Mrs. Bernick's cousin.

Doctor Rorlund, a schoolmaster.

Dina Dorf, a young girl living with the Bernicks.

Krap, the Consul's chief clerk.

Aune, the Consul's foreman.

Merchants, Ladies, Townspeople, Sailors, Steam-Boat Passengers, Etc.

The setting is a large room in the Bernick house looking out upon their garden.

PILLARS OF SOCIETY

TEXTUAL ANALYSIS

ACT ONE

While ladies of the small coastal town sew and Doctor Rorlund reads, Krap reprimands Aune for lecturing to the workmen on the evils of machinery and modern methods of work. The ladies and Dr. Rorlund discuss the harmful effects of too much gaiety, and drift to talk of the theatre and a party of actors who came to the town years ago. At that time Mrs. Bernick's brother Johan was involved with the wife of an itinerant actor and later was found to be guilty of embezzlement in the Bernick firm. Johan and his half sister Lona went to America.

Later Dr. Rorlund exacts a promise from Dina that she will, when the time comes, consent to be his wife. At this point Consul Bernick and three merchants enter from the Consul's office. Bernick makes it known that they have now approved the building of the railroad that they so violently opposed on moral grounds the previous year.

Olaf, the Bernicks' son, comes in saying that a circus company and other passengers have debarked at the dock. Lona and Johan are among them.

PILLARS OF SOCIETY

TEXTUAL ANALYSIS

ACT TWO

....

Bernick and his wife are upset about the return of Johan and Lona because the old scandal is being raked up again. Their discussion is interrupted by the entrance of Aune who is having great difficulty accepting new methods of work.

Bernick insists that repairs on the Indian Girl, an American ship, be completed in two days or the foreman will be dismissed. After Aune leaves, Hilmar Tonnesen comes in to inform them that the whole town is talking of Johan and Lona and the scandal. Consul Bernick orders Mrs. Bernick and Hilmar to be kind to them. Johan and Lona enter with Dina and Olaf. When Lona and Bernick are alone their conversation discloses that at one time they were in love. Lona refers to a "threefold lie" toward her, Bernick's wife, and Johan. His only excuse is that by lying he saved the house of Bernick, his family business. Lona wants him to confess his guilt, but he refuses.

Dina agrees to go to America with Johan, but Rorlund informs her that it was Johan who was involved in the scandal with Dina's mother. Rorlund accuses Johan of having stolen funds from the Bernicks' strongbox. Johan appeals to Bernick, but the Consul remains silent and goes off to a meeting about the railway.

PILLARS OF SOCIETY

TEXTUAL ANALYSIS

ACT THREE

....

Olaf has just been punished for sneaking out of the house and going to sea in a fishing boat. Bernick is upset as Krap enters and informs him that the Indian Girl, faultily repaired by Aune, is almost sure to sink. After Krap leaves, Hilmar Tonnesen informs Bernick of a rumor that someone is buying up all of the property along the proposed branch line of the railway. The public is indignant.

When Lona returns, Bernick explains that he was not guilty of stealing from his mother's cash box for there was no cash to steal. Bernick had helped to spread the rumor to prevent doubts from arising about the solidity of the firm. Johan asks Bernick to clear up all the lies so he can marry Dina and live in the town. Karsten Bernick refuses and tells them it is he who has bought all of the properties along the railway and that his associates will receive a fifth of the profits. He tells Johan that for Bernick's good as well as the town's he must be silent. Johan says that for now he will not speak. He will return to America on the Indian

Girl the next day, settle his affairs, and come back to marry Dina. Johan informs Bernick that he has two letters in which the latter admits to the fraud and that he will produce them when he returns.

Once again Bernick informs Aune that the Indian Girl must be ready to sail the next day or he will be dismissed. A heavy storm is expected, but still Bernick is determined to put the ship to sea.

Doctor Rorlund hears Johan and Dina make marriage plans and announces that Dina has promised to agree to be his wife when the time comes. Johan becomes angry and threatens to crush all upon his return.

PILLARS OF SOCIETY

TEXTUAL ANALYSIS

ACT FOUR

....

One of the local merchants informs Bernick that there is to be a great celebration in his honor, but the Consul is displeased. Johan is still determined to sail on board the Indian Girl. Olaf sneaks off to the pier under the pretense of saying goodbye to Johan. Unable to tolerate the idea of being engaged to Rorlund, Dina runs off to Johan. Martha and Lona are left and Martha tells Lona that she loves Johan.

Later Lona and Bernick are alone. He is still spinning excuses about why he cannot confess his guilt. The only reason, he says, is that he must leave a great inheritance for his son Olaf. Bernick then finds out that Dina and Johan have sailed, but not on the Indian Girl. He tries to stop the ship, but is too late. It is then he finds out that Olaf has run away aboard the Indian Girl. Mrs. Bernick, with the aid of Aune, locates him and Aune orders the ship not to sail until the next day.

The crowds come to praise Bernick and he makes a public confession. The property that only he and his friends were to share is now to be divided among the town. He then gives Aune sufficient time to make all of the repairs on the Indian Girl and Aune compromises in agreeing to make the repairs with the new machines.

Bernick feels a new respect for women and says that they are the pillars of society. Lona corrects him by saying that Truth and Freedom are the Pillars of Society.

Comment

Although the drama is primarily concerned with Consul Bernick's eventual confession and reformation of character, Ibsen provides a number of lesser plots to hold his audience's attention and to create suspense. In the first act, the return of the scandalous Johan and his half sister Lona makes the audience expect some interesting developments.

In the second act, Lona's disclosure of her earlier love affair with Bernick and the "threefold lie" leads us to expect that the Consul himself is involved in the embezzlement charged to his brother-in-law. But any further disclosures are delayed by Johan's lack of insistence and Bernick's evasiveness.

The third act is productive of much more suspense. How long will Johan remain silent? Will the two incriminating letters he made public? Will the Indian Girl put to sea and sink? Will Johan crush Rorlund upon his return? Will Bernick finally confess his guilt?

Ibsen adds more suspense in the last act. Johan and Dina plan to sail on the doomed ship and Olaf has just secreted himself on board. Bernick still hedges about confessing his guilt. When he finally does, his motivation is questionable. It is true that he has just experienced a series of shocks. Johan and Dina almost sailed on the Indian Girl; Olaf was rescued from it, and the sailing delayed just in time. In a truly generous mood, Lona tore up the incriminating letters before him. Bernick's confession nevertheless comes at an opportune time for himself. He admits his guilt before the assembled citizens' delegation, but he mentions only enough to clear Johan's name, and in such a manner that he gains in stature and popularity. The final line of the play embodies Ibsen's main **theme**, that the real "Pillars of Society" are Truth and Freedom, not any one individual.

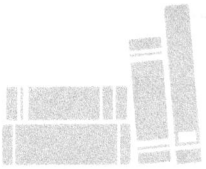

ROSMERSHOLM

INTRODUCTION

In this play, written in 1886, Ibsen continues the emphasis on symbolism and character analysis that marks *The Wild Duck*. *Rosmersholm* carries the method a great deal further, to the extent that the entire play depends more upon the successive developments in the inner state of the main character, Rebecca West, than upon any external events. The main plot of the play is concerned with Rebecca's gradual conversion from her freethinking selfish ways to a more truly liberal and noble view of life. Ibsen almost entirely relinquishes comedy in this play, because the joyless surroundings of *Rosmersholm* admit of no laughter. Social **satire** is present, in the stuffily conservative Kroll and the unprincipled liberal Mortensgaard, but little or no laughter. The tragic intensity of the piece is thus heightened by its somber tone, as well as by the recurrent image of the "white-horse" of death.

CHARACTERS

Johannes Rosmer, of Rosmersholm, former clergyman of the parish.

Rebecca West, his housekeeper.

Rector Kroll, his brother-in-law (Rector here means headmaster of a school).

Ulric Brendel, formerly Rosmer's tutor.

Peter Mortensgaard (pronounced Mortensgore), once a schoolteacher, now the editor of a liberal paper.

Madame Helseth, assistant to Miss West.

The setting is Rosmersholm, an ancient family seat near a small town on the west coast of Norway. Acts One, Three, and Four take place in the living room; Act Two in Rosmer's study.

ROSMERSHOLM

TEXTUAL ANALYSIS

ACT ONE

Rebecca West and Madame Helseth discuss the footbridge outside, where, as we soon learn, the late Mrs. Rosmer committed suicide. Rebecca is crocheting a large white shawl. Rector Kroll visits them and comments on her devotion to Rosmer, as well as to her late foster-father, Doctor West. Rosmer comes in and tells Kroll how they talk about his deceased wife Beata every day, as if she were still present. Kroll laments the existence of a secret liberal society at his school, led by his own children. He defends his extremely conservative position as the only right one and refers contemptuously to Mortensgaard, the editor of the liberal paper, "The Beacon." He asks Rosmer to edit a new conservative paper, or at least to lend the great old name of Rosmer of Rosmersholm to assure the success of the venture. Their conversation is interrupted by the arrival of the alcoholic tramp Ulric Brendel, Rosmer's former tutor. Brendel asks about the largest hall available nearby and announces his intention of delivering several lectures on the topic of emancipation. As he leaves he borrows money and a suit of clothes from Rosmer.

The latter then tells Kroll that he no longer believes in the conservative point of view. He is now a liberal and desires to emancipate the people by purifying and elevating their minds. He left the church because he no longer believes the religion of his ancestors. Infuriated, Kroll leaves, threatening that Rosmer must take the consequences of his defection.

ROSMERSHOLM

TEXTUAL ANALYSIS

ACT TWO

Rebecca tells Rosmer that she has sent a letter to Mortensgaard asking him to take care of Brendel. Kroll comes in complaining about her correspondence with the disreputable editor, and he interrogates Rosmer closely on the late Mrs. Rosmer's motives for suicide. Kroll mentions a letter she wrote to him, in which she said that she had not long to live, "for Johannes must marry Rebecca at once." The letter then alluded to the white horse of Rosmer, an apparition of the dead often seen at Rosmersholm. Kroll suspects Rosmer and Rebecca and accuses them of free love as well as of free thought. He finally appeals to Rosmer not to publish any of his new ideas, since Rosmersholm has always been a symbol of conservatism.

The next visitor is the editor Mortensgaard, who cautions Rosmer not to admit his loss of faith publicly, because that would alienate too many liberals as well as conservatives. He reminds Rosmer that the latter, when pastor, was responsible for the editor's dismissal from his position as schoolteacher.

Mortensgaard advises Rosmer to look into his own conscience and then tells him of a letter he received from the late Mrs. Rosmer, in which she denied any reports of Rosmer's loss of faith or sinful deeds.

All this while, Rebecca has been listening from behind a curtain. Rosmer asks what could have been the cause of his wife's suicide, and Rebecca evades the topic. He can no longer pursue his goal of liberating the souls of men, because his own soul feels restrained by his loss of innocence. He sees only one solution: to build a new life for himself. He asks Rebecca to marry him, but she, after an involuntary cry of joy, refuses, threatening to throw herself off the footbridge into the millrace below if the subject ever comes up again.

ROSMERSHOLM

TEXTUAL ANALYSIS

ACT THREE

Madame Helseth tells Rebecca how at Rosmersholm children never cry and people never laugh. A glance at some of the personal insults in the new conservative paper, "The County News," prompts Rosmer to confess to Rebecca his guilty feelings about his wife's death. He again dwells upon his inability to purify and elevate people's minds because of his own loss of innocence. After Rosmer goes for a walk Kroll comes to have a talk with Rebecca. He accuses her of designing to take over the Rosmer household and then gain Rosmer's love. Kroll then informs her that Doctor West, her supposed foster-father, was really her father. Her reaction is unaccountably emotional. He shows her how her own feelings on the score of her illegitimacy are far less damaging to her than Rosmer's sensitivity over his loss of faith is to him. Completely shaken, Rebecca then confesses to Rosmer and Kroll her guilt in Mrs. Rosmer's death. By careful insinuation she gradually persuaded Mrs. Rosmer to do away with herself for her husband's benefit. Rosmer goes to town with Kroll, and Rebecca, with an **allusion** to the white horses of Rosmersholm, has Madame Helseth pack her trunk.

ROSMERSHOLM

TEXTUAL ANALYSIS

ACT FOUR

Madame Helseth tells Rebecca that it is shameful of Rosmer not to marry her under the circumstances. Rebecca is ready to leave, but Rosmer returns. He blames her for using him, but she confesses how at first she loved him passionately, then gradually she was overcome by the spirit of Rosmersholm. Her will, once free, now has become infected by Rosmersholm. She has been ennobled by the Rosmer view of life, but her happiness is destroyed. Nevertheless, Rosmer's faith in himself and in her is gone. He asks for proof of her love. At this moment Brendel enters to pay his respects and take his final leave, since he is disillusioned with life and ready to give it up. His parting words are that Rosmer will achieve victory only by a sacrifice on the part of Rebecca. Inspired by Brendel's suggestion, Rosmer tells her that his faith can be restored only by her taking the same way his wife did. Rebecca quietly agrees, but Rosmer at first does not believe her capable of the deed. When he sees that she is in earnest, he joins her, and they go hand in hand out toward the footbridge over the millrace. As they go out the door Rosmer says, "Now we two are one." They wed in death.

Comment

The large white shawl at the beginning of the play is symbolic of the Rosmersholm view of life: a cold, joyless attachment to the past which finally overcomes Rebecca. This dead, lifeless aspect of the place is also represented by the late Mrs. Rosmer, whose marriage Rebecca describes as gloomy, and by Rosmer himself, who lacks the emotional vitality to apply his liberal ideals to action.

Rebecca herself undergoes a subtle psychological change that is already nearly complete at the beginning of the play. Originally an emancipated woman with extremely advanced ideas learned from her freethinking foster-father, step by step she comes more and more under the influence of Rosmer. Through him and her love for him, her character is transformed into something more womanly yet tragic. Her development is not really completed until her confessions: the first to both Kroll and Rosmer, the second and more intimate to Rosmer alone. The first of these is prompted by Kroll's revelation of her true parentage. Rebecca's nearly violent reaction suggests what is nowhere in the play stated, that her relationship to the Doctor may have involved incest. If this is true, then not only her reaction here but also her subsequent confession and suicide appear better motivated, since the shock of such a revelation would be a sufficient catalyst (activating agent) for her other emotions, especially her love for Rosmer, to bring about her tragic end.

The second confession affords a truer picture of Rebecca's relationship to Rosmer than the first. At this point, through her confession, she comes to a realization of herself, of her guilt as well as of her love. With the joylessness yet ennoblement of this view of herself, Rebecca has indeed followed the Rosmer way. What is left for her now and for Rosmer as well is only atonement, through which the two at last find joy, because they at once both expiate their guilt and unite themselves. The inexorably joyless House of Rosmer has triumphed, but in the victory its family line dies out.

JOHN GABRIEL BORKMAN

INTRODUCTION

Ibsen's last play but one, *John Gabriel Borkman* (1896), is the tragedy of a financier who like Bernick in *Pillars of Society* jilted a woman to marry her sister. Here the resemblance ends, since Borkman then proceeded to embezzle huge sums from his bank until he was finally detected and imprisoned. The action of the play involves Borkman himself, now a broken, self-deluded, but still defiantly hopeful old man, and the twin sisters who battle for the affections of Borkman's son Erhart. Like *Rosmersholm*, it is a tragedy, but it is the tragedy of a colossal egomaniac rather than of a mild-mannered idealist.

CHARACTERS

John Gabriel Borkman, formerly director of a bank.

    Mrs. Gunhild Borkman, his wife.

    Erhart Borkman, their son, a student.

    Miss Ella Rentheim, Mrs. Borkman's twin sister.

Mrs. Fanny Wilton, a divorcee.

Vilhelm Foldal (pronounced Wilhelm), a minor government clerk.

Frida Foldal, his daughter.

Mrs. Borkman's Maid.

The setting is the Rentheim family estate near Christiania (now Oslo) on a winter evening. There is no time lapse between acts.

JOHN GABRIEL BORKMAN

TEXTUAL ANALYSIS

ACT ONE

The great part of this act is taken up by a dramatic dialogue between the two sisters, who hate each other as passionately as they once both loved Borkman. Through their conversation nearly all of the **exposition** is presented. Borkman's ruin and imprisonment are outlined. His son Erhart was raised by Ella, who some time before the beginning of the play returned him to her sister. Mrs. Borkman boasts of her son's mission to reestablish the family name. As the two women talk, they hear the footsteps of Borkman himself, who daily since his release eight years before has paced up and down the room above, never once going outside, and visited only by the clerk Foldal and the Foldals' daughter Frida. During the entire eight years, Mrs. Borkman has never spoken to her husband.

Erhart enters and is kind to Ella despite all of his mother's efforts to poison his mind against his aunt. Mrs. Wilton then comes in and invites Erhart to a party at the Hinkels'. Mrs.

Borkman insists that he stay home, but within a few minutes he follows Mrs. Wilton to the party. The two sisters agree on only one thing: each would sooner see Erhart go with Mrs. Wilton rather than with the other.

JOHN GABRIEL BORKMAN

TEXTUAL ANALYSIS

ACT TWO

In a lengthy conversation with Foldal, Borkman explains his version of his ruin. Once a lowly miner's son, he was on the verge of profiting from his huge investments and returning all of the appropriated funds to the bank when the lawyer Hinkel, at whose home his son is now visiting, betrayed and ruined him. Borkman is certain, however that people will soon come to restore him to power and glory. Foldal, too, has his delusions. He believes that his daughter Frida will become a musician, that his unpublished tragedy will some day be famous, and that somewhere in the world there are good women. Borkman is unable to believe the last.

Ella Rentheim then enters. She reproaches Borkman for having jilted her years before. All he can think of is that her refusal to marry Hinkel led the latter to denounce him. He reminds her that only his care to leave her securities untouched at the bank saved her fortune. He then admits that he had loved her, but found it necessary to sacrifice her so that Hinkel would help to make him Bank Director. Ella tells him that in deserting her he destroyed both her capacity to love and his own, and ruined the life of Gunhild whom he married but never loved. She announces her intention of leaving her fortune to Erhart, provided the latter change his name to Rentheim. At this moment Mrs. Borkman breaks in upon them, declaring that Erhart's mission is to bring honor once more to the Borkman name.

JOHN GABRIEL BORKMAN

TEXTUAL ANALYSIS

ACT THREE

As soon as Mrs. Borkman leaves, Ella brings Borkman downstairs to come to an understanding with his wife. His explanation is that he has sinned only against himself and his wife and son. His greatest mistake, he says, was not immediately going into the world after his release and making another fortune. He complains that only one person ever understood him, and that was long ago. Her has never loved anyone or anything but power, and he will now go out and remake his fortune. Mrs. Borkman again insists upon her son's mission to rebuild the Borkman reputation.

Erhart then enters, and he is asked by his mother to remember his mission, by Ella to come home with her, and by his father to join him in his new life and work. Erhart refuses all three and insists that he must live his own life. He calls in Mrs. Fanny Wilton, with whom, although she is a divorcee and seven years his senior, he intends to elope. The young Foldal girl, Frida, will also go with them, ostensibly to study music. As Mrs. Wilton ironically puts it, it will be well for them both if Erhart has someone to fall back on when he is tired of her. The young ones leave.

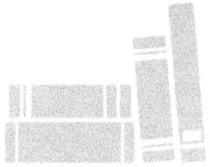

JOHN GABRIEL BORKMAN

TEXTUAL ANALYSIS

ACT FOUR

ACT FOUR, SCENE ONE

Act Four, Scene One (outside the Rentheim home). Mrs. Borkman rushes out to recall her son, who has already left in a sleigh with Mrs. Wilton and Frida. Ella and Borkman follow to dissuade her. They listen to the sound of sleigh bells fading in the distance, then Mrs. Borkman goes inside, Ella tries to bring Borkman inside, but he refuses to return within walls; he wants to stay in the open air and look for his "hidden treasures." Foldal then comes along, anxious to say goodbye to his daughter at Mrs. Wilton's before she leaves on her journey. He is so happy when he is told that she has already left on the big sleigh with silver bells that he forgets all about his foot being injured when he was struck by the same sleigh a few moments earlier. He hobbles off to tell the good news to his wife. Borkman then walks off through the snow-covered woods with Ella following close behind him.

ACT FOUR, SCENE TWO

Act Four, Scene Two (an open space at the edge of a plateau). Borkman looks out over the mountains and valleys and sees a vision of factories, all part of his imaginary great kingdom. The onetime miner turned financier sees veins of metal in the rocks, "treasures yearning for light." He cries out to them, "I love, love, love you." Ella again reminds him how in trading her love for power he murdered her "love-life." She declares that he will never win his "cold dark kingdom." Sinking, he feels an ice-hand at his heart, but then murmurs that it is "a metal hand." Mrs. Borkman then comes along with the maid, looking for her husband. The two sisters finally hold hands over the body of the man that both loved. Ella says: "We two shadows-over the dead man."

Comment

John Gabriel Borkman is essentially the tragedy of a man who devoted himself unflinchingly to the attainment of wealth and power and, in so doing, destroyed his own ability to love as well as that of the only woman he ever loved, Ella Rentheim. Since Ibsen usually equates the ability to love with the power to live, as in *Peer Gynt* and *Ghosts*, it is correct to conclude that Borkman has thus destroyed his true life. What he has left to sustain him after his ruin is a life-lie, a dream of being restored to wealth and power. His life-lie is comically paralleled by the optimistic delusions of the insignificant little clerk Foldal.

Also left only with a life-lie is Mrs. Borkman, who lives only in her mission for her son. While Borkman reaches almost tragic proportions in his colossal delusions, Mrs. Borkman is too icy, hard, unloving, and unforgiving to arouse much sympathy.

Of the two women, Ella Rentheim has a dignity entirely in keeping with the tragic tone of the play. Although she, like her sister, compensates for her emotional frustrations by their mutual hatred, Ella still maintains a degree of sympathy, both for Erhart and for Borkman, that is completely lacking in her sister Gunhild.. In addition, Ella's fatal disease that has brought her near death also contributes to making her character more sympathetic.

Critical opinion of the play varies considerably. It has often been considered faulty, especially by earlier critics. The chief objections to the piece are three. First, its action is too static; too much time is devoted to dialogue. Second, the mood is heavily oppressive. Third, the character of Borkman is too demented to be a tragic **protagonist** (chief character). On the credit side, this play is written with an intensity and vigor of expression at least equal to that of *The Master Builder*. Like that play, *John Gabriel Borkman* is a deeply emotional and thought-provoking study of defeat.

CRITICAL COMMENTARY

Toward the end of his career Ibsen remarked on the thematic continuity of his plays, and he insisted that they be studied as a group rather than separately. A brief survey of Ibsen's major plays will bear out the truth of his contention.

His two early dramas *Brand* (1886) and *Peer Gynt* (1867) deal with opposing but complementary themes. Both heroes are concerned with self-realization and both fail until the very end to come to grips with their own personalities. Brand finally sees his tragic fault in the very last scene, while Peer Gynt in the last act begins to perceive that he has never yet developed a self to realize.

In *Pillars of Society* (1877), Ibsen attacks the lies and falsehoods upon which society is reared, and in his next play takes up a specific example of this evil in society, contemporary views on marriage and womanhood. Thus *A Doll's House* (1879) shocked his contemporaries when Nora left her husband to find herself.

A variation of the **theme** of the above plays is treated in *Ghosts* (1881) when Ibsen describes the lies that bolster society as "ghosts" or dead ideas and beliefs out of the past, which throttle man's right to "joy of life." In this moving tragic drama, it was not so much his **theme** as his subject matter of venereal disease that outraged so many of his contemporaries.

The reception afforded *Ghosts* induced the author to write a quick reply. The result was an effectively fast-paced comedy, *An Enemy of the People* (1882). The same **theme** of outmoded ideas and beliefs was here presented, linked with the important corollary that the compact majority who believes in these ideas is always wrong; Ibsen thereby lost the support of the liberal party in Norway, at that time the most popular political group.

Not entirely satisfied with his portrait of the idealistic reformer Doctor Stockmann in *An Enemy of the People*, Ibsen produced a corrective or antidote in *The Wild Duck* (1884) in which he presents another idealist, Gregers Werle, who in his quest to bring truth to the Ekdal home only ruins what he seeks to elevate. In this play Ibsen, through the character of Doctor Relling, presents the idea that illusions are important for people to maintain their happiness or what Ibsen earlier calls "joy of life" (*Ghosts*). Thus every man is entitled to his life-lie.

Beginning with the next play, *Rosmersholm* (1886), Ibsen discards his social messages and turns in earnest to what he has already been doing well, the matter of psychological analysis of character. In this play he again concerns himself with the realization of self, but here he restricts the general **theme** to a specific study of what in Rebecca West might be termed excessive individualism. The subsidiary **theme** of the life-lie briefly flares up in the lesser characters of the conservative Kroll and the liberal Mortensgaard.

The same general **theme** of self-realization forms the basis of *Hedda Gabler* (1890). Hedda, even more than Rebecca West, suffers from excessive individualism. In this objective drama,

Ibsen presents one of his finest and keenest analyses of feminine character.

Individualism is again the **theme** of *The Master Builder* (1892), in which Halvard Solness seems unable to check his ruthless all-consuming ambition. A secondary **theme** is that of the responsibility of an artist or other creative person to his art. Solness thus sacrifices his own life as well as his wife's for his art. Added to this is the **theme** of defeat.

The final play considered at present is against devoted to the **theme** of excessive individualism. *John Gabriel Borkman* (1896) is like *The Master Builder* not only in this respect but also with regard to the minor **themes** of the creative artist and defeat.

In this brief review a number of basic **themes** have been noted which Ibsen touches upon again and again. Some of his principal **themes** are:

Self-realization, as in *Brand, Peer Gynt, A Doll's House.*

1. Quest for truth, as in *Brand, The Wild Duck.*

2. Joy of life, a subsidiary but important **theme** in *Ghosts, The Master Builder.*

3. Life-lie, a major **theme** in *The Wild Duck*; a minor theme (unstated as such) in *Peer Gynt, John Gabriel Borkman.*

4. Truth and Freedom as opposed to established conventions, in *An Enemy of the People, A Doll's House, Pillars of Society.*

5. Outmoded ideas and beliefs as poisonous, in *Ghosts, An Enemy of the People*.

Excessive individualism, in *Rosmersholm, Hedda Gabler, The Master Builder, John Gabriel Borkman*.

6. Artist's responsibility to his art, in *The Master Builder, John Gabriel Borkman*; by extension, also applicable to *Brand*.

Ibsen was most famous in his own day for his ringing denunciation of moral and social evils. Today he is not admired only as a moralist, but as a dramatist of the first rank. His influence upon modern drama is enormous. As creator and popularizer of the drama of ideas (or problem play) he deserves the greatest credit. Today, however, he is studied not so much for his influence as for his brilliant psychological analysis of character. It is this achievement more than any other that makes Ibsen's dramas continue to be read and produced up to the present day.

ESSAY QUESTIONS AND ANSWERS

Question: What are some of the moral and social evils which Ibsen attacked?

Answer: The one moral evil Ibsen attacked more than any other is selfishness. In *Brand* (1866), he depicts a self-centered Dean and Schoolmaster, both of whom are more interested in maintaining their positions than in performing any useful work. Ibsen's strongest denunciation of selfishness appears in another early play, *Peer Gynt* (1867). Here the motto of the trolls, which Peer religiously follows, is "Troll, to yourself be enough."

In the social plays, there are a number of selfish characters. In the first of these dramas, *Pillars of Society* (1877), Bernick stands out among other self-centered citizens as the ascme of self-interest, for he ruins his brother-in-law to advance himself. Another good example from this play is the double-dealing over the support of a new railroad line. As long as the railroad threatens to compete with the town's business of shipping, Bernick and the other leading citizens oppose it violently on moral grounds. As soon as the railroad is realigned so as to enrich the town rather than compete with it, all of the citizens, with Bernick as chief profit-maker at their head, approve of it wholeheartedly.

The second major target for Ibsen was the moral and social evil of outmoded ideas and beliefs. *Ghosts* (1881) is primarily devoted to this problem, as is *An Enemy of the People* one year later. The **theme** reappears in later plays, particularly in *Rosmersholm* (1886), where the ancient house of Rosmersholm, the symbol of entrenched ideas and opinions, oppresses the soul of Rosmer and eventually wins over the hitherto free will of Rebecca West.

Question: Describe some of the techniques by means of which Ibsen analyzes character.

Answer: Ibsen's chief technique in analyzing character is the gradual unfolding of past events. This is done for two purposes: (1) to inform his audiences step by step of the nature of each character; (2) to bring about significant development in character either by the disclosure of hitherto unknown facts from the past or by the revaluation of known facts. An example of the first his purpose is the manner in which Ibsen through his **exposition** gradually lets audience know what Nora Helmer is really like in *A Doll's House*. The second purpose needs more explanation. When in Rosmersholm, Rebecca West is suddenly informed that Doctor West, whose mistress she probably was, was her real father, she, under the pressure of the emotional shock, makes two confessions of her guilt. By so doing she gains rather than loses in tragic stature.

An example of the revaluation of the past is Mrs. Alving's realization at the end of the second act of *Ghosts* that her own cold, passionless sense of duty, with which she was brought up, was as much responsible for the failure of her marriage to Captain Alving as was the latter's irresponsible joy of life.

A second technique Ibsen sometimes uses to describe character is through action, as in *Hedda Gabler*, where Hedda's dangerous play with her pistols clearly points up the destructive aspects of her extremely neurotic character. In *An Enemy of the People*, Doctor Stockmann's brisk and airy dance with his wife at the end of the first act affords a good estimate of his bright, optimistic nature.

A third technique which Ibsen uses with effectiveness is the description of characters by others in the play. In *Rosmersholm*, Brendel describes the liberal editor Mortensgaard as one who is "capable of living his life without ideals." In *An Enemy of the People*, the editor Hovstad describes his printer Aslaksen as "chicken-hearted" and "a coward." Ibsen occasionally uses this device to describe both the speaker and the person spoken of. For instance, in *The Wild Duck*, Gregers Werle's insistence upon Hialmar Ekdal's noble and childlike mind tells us more about Gregers' idealistic but deluded character than it does about the shallow, selfish, and lazy Ekdal.

Question: Give some examples of Ibsen's use of symbolism to intensify his dramas.

Answer: In *Brand*, Ibsen uses the symbol of the little church on which the sun never shines to represent both the joylessness of Brand's fierce dedication and the spiritual littleness of his countrymen. Another symbol even more closely associated with Brand's tragedy is the hawk, which the gypsy Gerd sees and wishes to destroy. This symbol probably represents a harsh or even cruel element in Rand's quest for his ideal all or nothing. His inability to see the hawk until the very end of the play is indicative of his failure until it is too late to perceive his own tragic flaw-his stern and joyless concentration on his ideal quest to the exclusion of all other considerations.

In *The Wild Duck*, Ibsen's symbol presents such a multiplicity of possible meanings that it is difficult to pick out any one as the central interpretation (see the Introduction to the play). No reading of the piece, however, can be consideration valid unless this symbol is taken into account.

After *The Wild Duck*, Ibsen relies more and more heavily upon symbolism. In the next play, *Rosmersholm*, chief symbol is the white horse of Rosmersholm, which represents the way in which the spirit of the place embraces and absorbs all around it. The fact that no one in Rosmersholm or in the surrounding district laughs is indicative of the extent to which the Rosmer spirit has a stranglehold upon all connected in any way with the ancestral home. This white-horse symbol is reinforced by Rebecca West's large white shawl, which represents, as she finishes crocheting it, her own gradual surrender to the joyless enervating spirit of Rosmersholm. Rosmersholm itself is another symbol, representing the lifeless old ideas and beliefs that have always ruled there.

Question: Can any of Ibsen's plays ever be classified as tragedies? Explain.

Answer: The first matter is to set up standards for the **genre** (literary type) of tragedy. Classical tragedy, according to Aristotle's definition, is a drama in which the **protagonist** (chief character), being a person of considerable importance socially or politically, and one who is also marked by some type of personal greatness, suffers a disaster as a result partly of some flaw in his nature and partly of a reversal of fortune. In some plays the reversal of fortune may be associated with a recognition or realization of the tragic flaw, as in Sophocles' tragedy Oedipus Rex. The outcome of the classical tragedy usually produces in the audience an emotional reaction, which Aristotle identified as pity or fear, and then effects a catharsis (satisfaction or release) of emotion. Many modern tragedies, on the other hand, do not have a great or important **protagonist**, but only a hero whose downfall is often effected by marshalling social and psychological forces against him. Critics are still arguing today over the question whether modern tragedies should properly be called by the name tragedy. The critical fury raged over Arthur Miller's Death of a Salesman is a good example.

Keeping the above matters in mind, one may proceed to a judgment of some of Ibsen's plays. Certain of his earlier and lesser known works, like *The Vikings of Helgeland*, definitely fit the classical definition of tragedy. After *Brand*, however, Ibsen restricts himself to bourgeois (middle-class) drama, which may be classified as tragedy only according to the modern definition. *Brand* is the last play which follows the classical manner, since the hero of this play possesses the personal greatness necessary for tragedy and suffers destruction as a result of his tragic flaw.

Among the social dramas only *Ghosts* stands out as a possible tragedy. Here the disaster is one of personal loneliness; for Mrs. Alving is left at the end of the play only with memories of a debauched husband and a paralytic son. Her tragedy is caused by a combination of social forces (dead ideas and beliefs) and psychological forces (her own inability to free herself from these lifeless ideas).

Among Ibsen's later plays, *The Master Builder* and *John Gabriel Borkman* most closely approach tragedy. Because of the monomaniac drive of the **protagonist** in each drama, they are certainly classifiable as tragedies, since the downfall of each man results in part from his tragic flaw, which in each case is a series of life-lies or delusions.

Question: What types of people does Ibsen satirize most in his plays?

Answer: As a writer of social plays dealing with nineteenth-century Norway, where there was no upper or noble class as such, but only a middle and a lower class, Ibsen is concerned largely with depicting middle-class characters. Merchants, manufacturers, tradesmen, landowners, lawyers, doctors, ministers, teachers, and government officials are the people of his plays. Of all the professions, only the doctors escape relatively unscathed. Even the alcoholic wreck Doctor Relling in *The Wild Duck* is sympathetically portrayed.

Schoolmasters and scholars, with few exceptions, come off very poorly. The exceptions are Arnholm (*The Lady from the Sea*) and Alfred Allmers (*Little Eyolf*). The rest get their full share of **satire**, especially the pedantic George Tesman (*Hedda Gabler*), Rorlund (*Pillars of Society*), and the narrow-minded Rector Kroll (*Rosmersholm*). Women teachers, however, are treated with full favor and great respect: for example, Martha Bernick (*Pillars of Society*) and Petra Stockmann (*An Enemy of the People*).

Ibsen hates lawyers, as the few that he allows to roam through his plays evidence: the hypocritical philistine Torvald Helmer (*A Doll's House*), the heartless sensualist Judge Brack (*Hedda Gabler*), and the unprincipled and self-seeking Stensgaard (*Love's Comedy*). Even lower than lawyers in Ibsen's opinion are politicians and journalists. These are always presented as selfish, dishonest turncoats, such as Hovstad and Billing (*An Enemy of the People*) and Mortensgaard (*Rosmersholm*). For Krogstad in *A Doll's House*, however, Ibsen has some slight sympathy, probably because he is only a part-time journalist.

Ibsen treats his clergymen alike, for he seems to consider them all as useless to society. His best cleric is Brand, who is definitely not intended as representative of the regular clergy. Even Brand is fanatical in his insistence on all or nothing and on suffering as beneficial. The rest of Ibsen's clergymen form a herd of sheep rather than shepherds. From the politic Dean in *Brand* to the herd-follower Manders in *Ghosts,* they are unthinking champions of narrow, inflexibly conservative morality. The degenerate Molvik (*The Wild Duck*) completes Ibsen's gallery of nearly worthless clergymen.

BIBLIOGRAPHY AND GUIDE TO FURTHER RESEARCH

GUIDE TO FURTHER RESEARCH

Any research paper should be based on good, reliable translations. A list of these follows. For further bibliographical information on Ibsen, the most accessible source is the annual bibliography in the May issues, under "Scandinavian VI. Norwegian Literature. Nineteenth Century." An old but still useful bibliography as far as it goes is Ina Ten Eyck Firkins, *Henrik Ibsen: a Bibliography,* New York: H. W. Wilson, 1921.

Plays By Henrik Ibsen

Catiline 1850

Warrior's Barrow, The 1850

Norma 1851

St. John's Eve 1853

Lady Inger of Ostraat 1855

Feast at Solhaug, The 1856

Olaf Liljekrans 1857

Vikings in Helgeland, The 1858

Love's Comedy 1862

Pretenders, The 1863

Brand 1866

Peer Gynt 1867

League of Youth, The 1869

Emperor and Galilean 1873

Pillars of Society 1877

Doll's House, A 1879

Ghosts 1881

Enemy of the People, An 1882

Wild Duck, The 1884

Rosmersholm 1886

Lady from the Sea, The 1888

Hedda Gabler 1890

Master Builder, The 1892

Little Eyolf 1894

John Gabriel Borkman 1896

When We Dead Awaken 1899

EDITIONS AND TRANSLATIONS OF IBSEN'S WORKS

Collected Works, tr. and ed. William Archer. 12 vols. New York: Scribner, 1908-1912. The standard complete English edition. Old and not altogether faithful to the original, it still rises to poetic vigor in the rendition of the later plays.

Correspondence of Henrik Ibsen, ed. Mary Morison. London: Hodder and Stoughton, 1905. Old but standard.

Ibsen: Letters and Speeches, ed. Evert Sprinchorn. New York: Hill and Wang, 1964. New and dependable.

Speeches and New Letters, tr. Arne Kildal. London: Frank Palmer, 1911. Old but standard.

The following are some of the modern translations available in paper-back editions, listed by translator:

Fjelde, Rolf. *Four Major Plays.* Signet Classic. (*A Doll's House, The Wild Duck, Hedda Gabler, The Master Builder*).

Forsyth, James. *Brand, a New Version.* Theatre Arts Books.

LeGallienne, Eva. *Six Plays by Henrik Ibsen.* Modern Library T24.

McFarlane, James W. *Ibsen: An Enemy of the People, The Wild Duck, Rosmersholm.* New York: Oxford University Press, 1961. The first issue of a projected new complete edition and translation of Ibsen. When finished, it will replace the Archer edition as the standard complete edition in English.

Meyer, Michael. *When We Dead Awaken and Three Other Plays.* Doubleday Anchor. (*The Lady from the Sea, The Master Builder, John Gabriel Borkman*).

___. *Hedda Gabler and Three Other Plays.* Doubleday Anchor. (*Pillars of Society, The Wild Duck, Little Eyolf.*)

___. *Brand.* Doubleday Anchor.

___. *Peer Gynt.* Doubleday Anchor. This and the three preceding editions are standard acting editions of Ibsen's major plays.

Paulson, Arvid. *The Last Plays of Henrik Ibsen.* Bantam Books HC94.

Sharp, R. Farquharson. *Four Great Plays by Ibsen.* Bantam Books HC 177. (*A Doll's House, Ghosts, An Enemy of the People, The Wild Duck*).

Watt, Peter. *Ghosts and Other Plays.* Penguin Books. (*A Public Enemy, When We Dead Awaken*).

BIOGRAPHICAL AND CRITICAL STUDIES

Bradbrook, M. C. *Ibsen the Norwegian.* London: Chatto and Windus, 1948. A good review of Ibsen's career as playwright, with emphasis on historical backgrounds.

Downs, Brian W. *Ibsen: the Intellectual Background.* Cambridge, England: Cambridge University Press, 1946. An excellent discussion of Ibsen's intellectual, social, and political backgrounds. Philosophy and politics are particularly well handled.

Downs, Brian W. *A Study of Six Plays by Ibsen.* Cambridge, England: Cambridge University Press, 1950. Some penetrating remarks on *Love's Comedy, Brand, Peer Gynt, A Doll's House, The Wild Duck,* and *The Master Builder.*

Heller, Otto. *Henrik Ibsen: Plays and Problems.* Boston: Houghton, Mifflin Company, 1912. Contains a brief biography and full essays on all of the major plays. Although outdated and uneven, this critical biography is still very important.

Jorgenson, Theodore. *Henrik Ibsen: a Study in Art and Personality.* Northfield, Minn., 1945. A straightforward work with considerable biographical material as well as detailed plot and character analyses. Rather weak in critical interpretation.

Knight, G. Wilson. *Henrik Ibsen.* New York: Grove Press, 1964. Like all of Professor Knight's criticisms, always brilliant and sometimes erratic. The result of a number of seminars in Ibsen conducted by the author, this book, despite its brevity, is a major contribution to modern Ibsen criticism.

Koht, Halvdan. *The Life of Ibsen,* tr. McMahon and Larsen. 2 vols. New York: W. W. Norton, 1931. Still the definitive biography of Ibsen.

Lavrin, Janko. *Ibsen: An Approach.* London: Methuen, 1950. An analysis based largely on the so-called new criticism of Cleanth Brooks and his followers, this book affords a good general introduction and some challenging criticisms of the plays.

Lucas, F. L. *The Drama of Ibsen and Strindberg.* New York: Macmillan, 1962. A good comparative study.

McFarlane, James Walter. *Ibsen and the Temper of Norwegian Literature.* London, 1960. A reasonably successful effort to place Ibsen in the stream of Norwegian literature.

Northam, John. *Ibsen's Dramatic Method.* London: Faber and Faber, 1953. An interesting study of the visual effects of Ibsen's plays, relying upon the stage directions. Also considers earlier manuscript drafts of the plays. Contains a good treatment of symbolism in the later plays.

Shaw, George Bernard. *The Quintessence of Ibsenism.* New York: Brentano's, 1912. A classic in its own right, this long essay tells us more about Shaw than Ibsen.

Tennant, P. F. D. *Ibsen's Dramatic Technique.* Cambridge, England: Bowes and Bowes, 1948. A study of Ibsen's settings, stage directions, exposition, plot, and **denouement** (ending).

Weigand, Hermann J. *The Modern Ibsen: A Reconsideration.* New York: Henry Holt and Co., 1925. Reprinted New York: E. P. Dutton, 1960, Dutton Paperback D54. Indispensable. Still the best critical volume on Ibsen in English. Mainly psychoanalytical in approach, it affords a brilliant exegesis of twelve plays, from *Pillars of Society* to *When We Dead Awaken.*

Zucker, A. E. *Ibsen the Master Builder.* London: Thornton Butterworth, 1930. A good short biography, with comparatively little criticism of the plays.

ESSAYS OR DISCUSSIONS DEALING WITH IBSEN:

The following volumes contain important

Balmforth, Ramsden. *The Problem-Play and its Influence on Modern Thought and Life.* New York: Henry Holt and Co., 1928.

Bentley, Eric. *In Search of Theatre.* New York: Alfred A. Knopf, 1953.

___. *The Playwright As Thinker.* New York: Reynal and Hitchcock, 1946. Reprinted Cleveland: World Publishing Co., 1963 (Meridian Paperback).

Brooks, Cleanth, ed. *Tragic **Themes** in Western Literature.* Yale University Paperback Y25. Contains a good essay by Konstantin Reichardt.

___. and Robert B. Heilman. *Understanding Drama.* London: Harrap, 1946.

Fergusson, Francis. *The Idea of a Theatre.* Princeton: Princeton University Press, 1949.

Gassner, John. *Masters of the Drama.* 3rd ed. rev. New York: Dover Publications, 1954.

Granville-Barker, Harley. *On Dramatic Method.* New York: Hill and Wang, 1963. A reprint of an old but still basic text on dramatic technique by a talented playwright.

James, Henry. *The Scenic Art: Notes on Acting and the Drama,* 1872-1901, ed. Allan Wade. New Brunswick: Rutgers University Press, 1948.

Lamm, Martin. *Modern Drama,* tr. Karin Elliott. New York: Oxford University Press, 1952.

Williams, Raymond. *Drama from Ibsen to Eliot.* London, 1952.

GENERAL BACKGROUNDS

Brown, John Mason. *The Modern Theatre in Revolt.* New York: W. W. Norton, 1929.

Chandler, Frank W. *Aspects of Modern Drama.* New York: Macmillan, 1914.

___. *Modern Continental Playwrights.* New York: Harper, 1931. Detailed accounts of a number of Ibsen's contemporaries and followers.

Clark, Barrett H. *A Study of the Modern Drama.* New York: Appleton-Century, 1938. A reliable general history.

Jorgenson, Theodore. *History of Norwegian Literature.* New York: Macmillan, 1933.

Lewisohn, Ludwig. *The Modern Drama.* New York: Huebsch, 1921. A discussion of modern developments in drama. Quite good on Ibsen.

Lukacs, George. *Studies in European **Realism**,* tr. Edith Bone. London: Hillway Publishing Co., 1950.

Stanton, Stephen S., ed. *Camille and Other Plays.* New York: Hill and Wang, 1957. (Mermaid Dramabook MD6.) Contains a brilliant introduction on the technique of the well-made play, as perfected by Eugene Scribe.

www.ingramcontent.com/pod-product-compliance
Lightning Source LLC
LaVergne TN
LVHW021701060526
838200LV00050B/2461